HIDDEN HISTORIES

Tales From Cathays Cemetery

Friends of Cathays Cemetery
Cardiff

Published by Friends of Cathays Cemetery

Designed by Daydream Education

Printed by Zenith Media, Pontypool

Acknowledgements

The Friends of Cathays Cemetery are grateful to the following, without whom the production of this book would not have been possible:

The Heritage Lottery Fund for the grant, which has underwritten the cost of publication.

The National Library of Wales, Glamorgan Archives, Cardiff Library, Midlothian Council Local History Library and, of course, the wealth of information available at the click of a button on the internet. Appropriate accreditations are given against individual items as they appear in the book.

Dr Julian Litten, a Cardiff Graduate, Researcher and Fellow of the Society of Antiquaries, for the Preface.

Cardiff Bereavement Services for their unstinting support for this enterprise and for all the activities of the Friends.

Members of the Friends who have undertaken the majority of the research and writing provided most of the illustrations and constructively reviewed drafts. Accreditations are given throughout the book. Special thanks go to the members of the Editorial Team, John Farnhill, Gordon Hindess, Paul Jones and Paul Nicholson, for bringing it all together.

Cover image: Episcopalian Chapel, viewed from the north – Gordon Hindess
Frontspiece: Celtic Cross in Section L – Gordon Hindess
Image facing page 1 – John Farnhill
All other full page images – Tracie Harper
Inside front and back cover photography – John Farnhill and Bereavement Services

ISBN: 978 0 9562786 1 6
Title: Hidden Histories Tales from Cathays Cemetery

About this Book

The tenth anniversary of the formation of the Friends of Cathays Cemetery in 2006 warranted a celebration of the group's achievements to date. Perhaps the most visible achievement is that the sadly neglected Victorian chapels have been made habitable and brought back into use, although there remains more to do. However, there are other achievements – a regular newsletter of acknowledged quality, a comprehensive and informative website, a weekly health walk and a full programme of guided walks and talks.

The Friends became a registered charity in 2010 with the following aims:

• To promote the conservation and protection of the infrastructure, monuments & buildings of Cathays Cemetery for the public benefit

• Likewise to promote the conservation and protection of the flora & fauna in the Cemetery

• To advance the education of the public in the history and heritage of the Cemetery

• To promote its importance as a conservation area and use as an educational resource.

The group also seeks to work with Cardiff Council and to promote the Cemetery as a haven for both reflection and remembrance.

Behind the scenes, research has populated a growing archive of information about the Cemetery and those buried in it and, in line with the last two of its aims, it is important to present this publicly in as many forms as possible. Therefore, what better way to mark the Friends' tenth anniversary, than to publish its second book, a companion to 'Cathays Cemetery Cardiff on its 150th Anniversary'. This book looks at a selection of people who have contributed to the history and heritage of Cardiff and its hinterland.

Contents

Preface

When Cathays Cemetery was established in 1859 it was to be the largest public cemetery in Wales and, indeed, it remains the third largest cemetery in the United Kingdom. It is the resting-place of Cardiff's gentry, of its Victorian and Edwardian coal and shipping magnates but, chiefly, it is the resting-place of thousands of its ordinary citizens: factory-workers, shop-workers, clerks, tradesmen and even that of its less fortunate sons and daughters.

A perambulation of its extensive grounds will make the visitor aware that, as with the great city of Cardiff itself, Cathays Cemetery also has its high town, its suburbs and its low-town. As conscious of society's boundaries in life so, too, did the cemetery have its favoured areas in death. Lining the pathways closest to the chapels can be found the brick graves and huge monuments of the city's grandees, whilst it is to the furthest regions of the cemetery, adjacent to the perimeter boundaries, that the lesser monuments are to be found.

For almost a hundred years Cathays was considered as the cemetery in which to be buried, but after World War II such feelings declined and, with the adoption of simpler forms of sculptural commemoration and, it has to be said, with the introduction of cremation as an alternative means of disposal, such cemeteries as Cathays went into decline. Its closure to new burials in 1986 saw its decline, becoming overgrown and unkempt, its chapels by Thomas & Waring of Cardiff, no longer required for their original purpose, falling into decay.

The resurrection of Cathays took place in 2006, when a small band of concerned volunteers, assisted by the city's Bereavement Services, established the Friends of Cathays Cemetery. As the overgrowth was cleared the impressive Victorian and Edwardian monuments began to reveal themselves. The chapels, once swathed in ivy, regained their elegant appearance, and Cathays Cemetery came to life again. This book tells the story of that challenge but, most of all, it relates the Victorian Way of Death which, though more elaborate than that which society accepts today is, nevertheless, a highly important facet of Cardiff's past.

Dr Julian W S Litten FSA

Rhagair

Pan sefydlwyd Mynwent Cathays ym 1859, hi fyddai mynwent fwyaf Cymru, ac yn wir, mae hi'n dal i fod y drydedd fwyaf yn y Deyrnas Unedig. Dyma fan gorffwys bonheddwyr Caerdydd, pendefigion glo a morio Oes Fictoria a'r Oes Edwardaidd, ond yn bennaf, dyma fan gorffwys miloedd o ddinasyddion Caerdydd: gweithwyr ffatri, gweithwyr siop, clerciaid, masnachwyr a hefyd ei meibion a merched llai ffodus.

Bydd taith o amgylch y tiroedd eang yn dangos i'r ymwelydd bod ucheldref, maestrefi ac iseldref yn Mynwent Cathays, fel sydd yng Nghaerdydd ei hun. Roedd pobl yr un mor ymwybodol o ffiniau cymdeithas tir y meirw â rhai tir y byw felly roedd ardaloedd penodol i'r fynwent hefyd. Ar ymylon y llwybrau agosaf at y capeli, mae beddau brics a chofebau enfawr mawrion y ddinas, ac yn y pellfannau, ger ffiniau'r fynwent y mae'r cofebau "llai pwysig".

Am bron i ganrif, Cathays oedd y fynwent o ddewis er mwyn claddu, ond wedi'r Ail Ryfel Byd, dirywiodd y ddelfryd wrth bobl ddechrau defnyddio cofebau cerflun symlach a'r dull newydd wedi angau, sef amlosgi. Gwaethygodd sefyllfa mynwentydd megis Cathays. Wedi iddi beidio â derbyn eirch newydd yn 1986, bu i'r fynwent ddirywio a thyfodd glaswellt a phlanhigion dros y beddau. Aeth y capeli, gan Thomas & Waring, Caerdydd, a'u pennau iddynt gan nad oedd pobl yn eu defnyddio bellach.

Cafodd Cathays ei adfywio yn 2006 pan sefydlwyd Cyfeillion Mynwent Cathays gan griw o wirfoddolwyr, a oedd yn bryderus am y sefyllfa, gyda chymorth Gwasanaethau Profedigaeth y ddinas. Wrth glirio'r tyfiant, datgelwyd y cofebau mawreddog o Oes Fictoria a'r Oes Edwardaidd. Cafodd y capeli, a fu dan orchudd o iorwg, eu hadfer i'w gogoniant gynt a daeth Mynwent Cathays eto'n fyw. Mae'r llyfr yn adrodd hanes yr her hon, ond yn fwy na dim, mae'n sôn am agwedd Oes Fictoria tuag at farwolaeth, sy'n rhan bwysig o orffennol Caerdydd, er na chydnabyddir hynny'n llawn heddiw.

Dr Julian W S Litten FSA

Plan of Old Cemetery

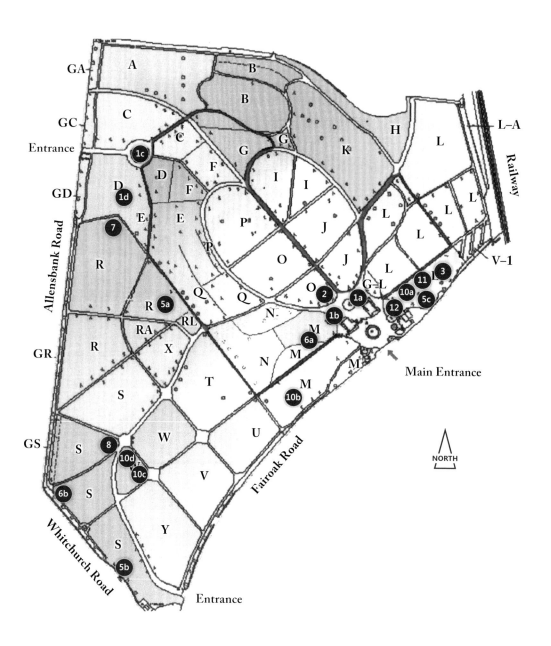

Location Key

Chapter/ Plan Reference	Feature or Grave	Plot Number
1a	Episcopalian Chapel	Not applicable
1b	Nonconformist Chapel	Not applicable
1c	Site of Former Catholic Chapel	Not applicable
1d	Maria Dolores de Pico	D 1022
2	John Batchelor	O 967
3	Dr Henry James Paine	L 1067
5 - see footnote	David and Thomas Jenkins	E-F 8975
5 - see footnote	William Pain	E-F 8955
5 - see footnote	William Henry Robson	E-F 8935
5 - see footnote	George Pingree	E-F 8932
5 - see footnote	Frank Langmaid	E-H 1260
5a	Thomas Collier	R 2479
5b	Samuel John Manfield	S 3465
5c	Thomas Jones	L 1365
6a	Archibald Hood	M 536
6b	Main Caledonian Society grave headstone	S 3395
7	James Mullin	R 13
8	William Harpur	S 1664
9 - see footnote	Bernard Bastable	E-H 2162
9 - see footnote	Windsor Phillips	E-F 8572
10a	Richard Cory (Bideford family)	L 1481
10b	John Cory Senior (Padstow family)	M 1257
10c	John Cory Junior (Padstow family)	W 1243
10d	James Herbert Cory - Baronet (Padstow family)	W 920
11	Charles Lafayette Hunter	L 1184
12	James Emerson Williams	L 1438

Footnote : Some graves mentioned in Chapters 5 and 9 are in the New Cemetery (north of Eastern Avenue), so do not appear on the Plan opposite.

CHAPTER ONE

History of the Cemetery

Today Cathays Cemetery, the largest in Wales, is surrounded by housing. Much of this is from the late 19th Century or afterwards, but when the cemetery was opened in 1859, it was on edge of a town whose population was growing rapidly as a result of the industrial revolution. The town's population rose from 1,870 in 1801 to 18,351 in 1851 and within a few years of the opening of the Cemetery it had reached 32,951 (1861). The acreage of the town increased and the density of population per acre grew with it.

It was this growth in population which triggered the need to find a solution to the overcrowding the traditional places of burial within Parish churchyards. As early as 1822 attempts were made to extend the churchyard of the two parishes, which made up Cardiff, but this was to prove but a short-term solution and in 1836 land was granted to the Council by Lord Bute in the hope that this would provide burial space for the foreseeable future. A year after the consecration of this new burial ground in 1848 there was an outbreak of cholera, which led to the deaths of 360 people in rapid succession, so filling the newly available land.

Whilst Cardiff's growth in numbers was proving difficult, nowhere was the problem more acute than in London where grisly stories of one burial disturbing the all too recent remains of another abounded and where the stench from some burial sites, including church crypts, became intolerable. It was recognised that there was a real and urgent need for reform and in 1852 Parliament passed the first of several Burial Acts under which church and chapel burial grounds could be closed to new burials and the local authorities could be constituted a Burial Board. This was the start of the Cemetery Movement. At first, these new cemeteries were privately run and represented something of a gamble. What was needed was the approval of the upper echelons of society to make them socially acceptable, indeed fashionable.

In 1854 Cardiff Town Council moved to close a number of old burial grounds and following the 1855 Burial Act, the Council was constituted a Burial Board on 30th Jan 1856 with the purpose of providing for requisite places of burial for the inhabitants of the parishes of St John and St Mary in the Borough of Cardiff. That same year more old burial grounds were deemed full and were closed to new burials. The Council now had to act to find a new site and in 1859 new land within the parish of St. John, the Baptist was purchased and consecrated.

The cemetery site covered some 30 acres and was from the outset intended not only to be a practical solution to the problem of finding a resting place for the deceased of

Cardiff but also a pleasant park for recreation. The grounds were landscaped and numerous specimen trees were planted along with flowerbeds so giving the cemetery the appearance of a country park, literally a garden of remembrance.

Within the park were constructed a number of buildings whose purpose was to serve the cemetery. Perhaps the most imposing of these are the funerary chapels, one Anglican the other non-conformist. These chapels were built to joint designs by Mr R G Thomas, an Architect who subsequently worked in Adelaide, and Mr Thomas Waring, Surveyor to the Board of Health of Cardiff. The chapels, which face the Fairoak Road entrance to the cemetery, were built in a Gothic-inspired style. The same architects also designed a Roman Catholic chapel, which had its own entrance from what we now know as Allensbank Road. The style chosen for this building was not Gothic but had a rather more modest, almost rural appearance. Unfortunately, neither the Catholic chapel nor the joint funerary chapels were especially well constructed and all needed frequent repair within years of their construction. Fortunately the Anglican and non-conformist chapels have survived, albeit only just, and in recent years have undergone refurbishment and restoration by Cardiff Council's Bereavement Services in association with Friends of Cathays Cemetery. The Catholic chapel was less fortunate and had to be demolished in 1986.

A model of the now demolished catholic chapel

Courtesy of Roger Martin

The 30 acres of the new cemetery proved to be adequate but the Council were aware that the population was continuing to grow and took the precaution of purchasing additional land, and additional 4 acres, three of which were consecrated the remaining acre being kept for non-conformist burial. The purchase was made in 1878 although the consecration of it did not take place until 1903. However, the Council continued to plan ahead and on 15th May 1879, the Town Clerk was instructed to write to Mr Corbett, Agent to the Bute Estate, that the additional land of 11 acres, which was the remaining land of Crwys Brychan Farm, was to be purchased from Lord Bute.

Because this land was not immediately needed for burials, but rather was being reserved for them, it was decided that it should be used as a temporary recreation ground. The decision was not without opposition, but following discussion the matter was decided and, an announcement appeared in the advertisement columns of the local Press on 18th July 1881, as below:

Borough of Cardiff Notice

The ground adjoining the Cemetery will be opened to the public for recreation purposes on and after Monday next, the 18th inst., between the hours of 8 a.m. and 9.30 p.m., daily. Free. By order, F.R. Greenhill, Clerk, Town Hall Cardiff, 15th July 1881.

By the time Cardiff's cemetery came to be opened, the movement was well established. Nonetheless, it cannot have been a bad thing that the first burial to be made in the cemetery was that of Maria Dolores de Pico, the daughter of the Spanish Consul.

Nicholas Davey & Paul Nicholson

CHAPTER TWO

John Batchelor (1820–1883)

John Batchelor was born in Newport in 1820 and, in 1843 came to Cardiff with his brother Sidney to set up a timber business, as Batchelor Bros. Initially they took over a yard on the bank of the River Taff at the lower end of St Mary Street and then, around 1854, moved to a new yard near the West Bute Dock. The company later added a slate business and subsequently opened timber yards in Cardiff, Merthyr and Aberdare. It was perhaps inevitable that John Batchelor should develop his business interests to include nautical elements, including a move into shipbuilding. He was one of a group of men who established the Mount Stuart Graving Dock.

Batchelor had a clear social conscience and his concerns led him to the radical wing of the Liberal Party. Between 1850 and 1859, he was a Liberal councillor for Cardiff South and in 1853/54, he served as Cardiff's Mayor. He was elected president of the Cardiff Liberal Association in 1869 and, as a devoted Congregationalist; he was responsible for the founding of a new chapel in Charles Street. Batchelor's range of interests was immense and he campaigned, tirelessly, against abuses such as slavery. Above all, he was concerned with education, serving as Chairman of the Cardiff School Board, but most especially municipal reform and was opposed to the vested interests of the Tories. He genuinely wanted to help people less fortunate than himself, and always sided with the underdog, a stance that brought him into regular conflict with the establishment.

Perhaps inevitably, John Batchelor's political activity brought him into conflict with the Bute family, who had significant land-holdings in Cardiff, had built many of the docks and were probably the most important and influential family in South Wales. There were many disputes, particularly with John Crichton-Stuart, the third Marquess. Partly as a way of circumventing Bute's control of the Welsh coal trade, Batchelor became involved in the creation of Penarth Docks, being appointed its director in 1856.

There are claims that the eventual collapse of Batchelor's business empire was down to various conspiracies by the Butes and their supporters. Whatever the reason, he lost money, his companies went into serious financial decline and, in 1873, and the company went into liquidation. However, John Batchelor still had many friends and supporters, who, after the collapse of his businesses, held a collection and were able to present him with the grand sum of £5,000 – equivalent to about £350,000 today. Batchelor continued to work as an agent until his death in 1883 but, as far as social reform and public acclaim were concerned, his glory days had gone.

It was on 23rd July 1886, some three years after his demise, that friends erected the statue of him in the Hayes. The sculptor, commissioned for a fee of £1000, was James Milo Griffiths, of London, and it was cast in bronze at the workshop of James More at Thames Ditton. The statue stands on a 9'6" high pedestal of Cornish granite weighing 12 tons. At the time of erection, the inscription had yet to be engraved.

If the statue was received by some with "the utmost satisfaction", it roused others to fury. The day after the unveiling the following appeared in the correspondence columns of the Western Mail:-

Our esteemed correspondent Censor suggests the following epitaph
for the Batchelor statue.

IN HONOUR OF
JOHN BATCHELOR
A NATIVE OF NEWPORT
WHO EARLY IN LIFE LEFT HIS COUNTRY FOR HIS COUNTRY'S GOOD
WHO ON HIS RETURN DEVOTED HIS LIFE AND ENERGIES TO
SETTING CLASS AGAINST CLASS
A TRAITOR TO THE CROWN, A REVILER OF THE ARISTOCRACY, A
HATER OF THE CLERGY A PANDERER TO THE MULTITUDE
WHO AS FIRST CHAIRMAN OF THE CARDIFF SCHOOL BOARD
SQUANDERED FUNDS TO WHICH HE HAD NOT CONTRIBUTED
WHO IS SINCERELY MOURNED BY UNPAID CREDITORS
TO THE AMOUNT OF
FIFTY THOUSAND POUNDS
WHO AT THE CLOSE OF A WASTED AND MISSPENT
LIFE DIED A DEMOGOGUE AND A PAUPER
THIS MONUMENT
TO THE ETERNAL DISGRACE OF CARDIFF
IS ERECTED
BY SYMPATHETIC RADICALS

The writer was Thomas H Ensor, a successful solicitor, staunch Conservative, and regular contributor to the paper under the name "Censor". In the same edition of the paper appeared the following letter, possibly written by the same hand.

Sir, if the authorities... desired to frighten away the fish-hawkers and Salvation Army loafers who make the Hayes their happy hunting ground, they could not have taken more effective measures than they have in erecting the hideous effigy now to be seen there. 'A thing of beauty is a joy forever' but John Batchelor "the old election hand" in a pair of oilskin leggings several sizes too large for him is certainly no ornament to Cardiff. The paper that the effigy clutches cannot, of course, be other than the late Mr. Batchelor's "petition in bankruptcy". Then the moral that the statue teaches all bad boys is obvious, "Mind everybody's business but your own, and your caricature will be set up in the back streets as a laughing stock for future generations".

It was signed "An Admirer Of High Art".

The South Wales Daily News of 28th July 1886 describes how sons of John Batchelor, Cyril and Llewellyn, had for some days met the train arriving from Penarth about 11 a.m. on which the editor of the Western Mail, Mr Henry Lascelles Carr, usually travelled. Rumours had spread and a crowd had gathered by the time Carr arrived. The brothers had sought both Carr and Ensor: Carr was just the unlucky one. The paper continues the story as follows:-

Approaching him when he was halfway between the Station and the Great Western Hotel, Mr. Cyril Bachelor seized him by the shoulder and shouted, "Your name is Carr, I believe?" Before the latter had time to reply Mr Cyril knocked off his hat and then excitedly exclaiming, "You are the cowardly fellow who has libelled my Father", he drew forth a dog whip, having a short handle and a long thick thong. Raising his strong right arm, he brought the lash down upon the shoulders of his cringing victim, who is said to have appealed for mercy, but whose cries went unheeded. Again and again, the thong twined round the body of the alleged libeller, who in sheer madness and pain closed with his assailant and thus prevented his arm from having full play. After some hugging in which Mr Batchelor freely used his fists Carr was thrown to the ground, but so tightly did he clutch the garments of his antagonist that he also fell, the latter however being the uppermost.

A vast crowd had by this time collected. After the two men had regained their feet besmeared with mud from head to foot, the editor of the Tory newspaper rapidly pulled off his coat and offered to fight either of the Batchelors. Mr. Llewellyn, who up to this time had been a passive spectator to the affray, then stepped forward and offered to oblige the pugilistic Mr. Carr, but the spectators interfered and both gentlemen were held back. Mr. Carr was in a short time hurried away to his office, and taking a cab the Messrs. Batchelor were driven to their place of business at the docks.

Later the same day, Mr. Morgan Morgan, acting for Carr, took out a summons for assault and the case was heard before a deputy stipendiary magistrate the following week. Following lengthy argument, the magistrate concluded that the assault had been proved, but was of a somewhat trifling nature and because of great provocation. The two Batchelor sons were fined a shilling (5p).

However, their prosecution in the magistrates court was not the end of the matter. The following year, the indictment of Thomas Ensor and Lascelles Carr for criminal libel came before the Nisi Prius Court in Cardiff. This case established a legal precedent, which aroused great interest nationwide. The judge concluded that libel on dead men is not indictable, saying "It is as safe to call one who died last year a liar and a murderer as it is to apply these epithets to Julius Caesar or Oliver Cromwell".

This precedent was to feature, many years later, in the defence of a Prime Minister's reputation. W E Gladstone devoted much time to saving what were then known as "fallen women". It is noted that Gladstone's habit was to talk to such women on the streets and to even visit them in their rooms. He quite understood what malicious minds would make of these practices and sure enough, slanderous allegations against him began in 1876, often in the form of unsigned letters. These continued after his death but it was not until 1925 that legal redress was sought. A Captain Peter Wright wrote, "Gladstone founded a great tradition ... in public to speak the language of the highest and strictest principle and in private to pursue and possess every sort of woman".

Mr. Gladstone's two sons, Henry and Viscount Gladstone (both in their seventies), were advised that a private

The statue of John Batchelor in the Hayes
Gordon Hindess

prosecution for libel against their dead father would fail, with the leading case of Regina versus Ensor and Lascelles Carr being cited. However, they felt that they could not let the slur pass unchecked, so they wrote to Wright, copying the letter to the newspapers, "Your garbage has come to our knowledge. You are a liar. Because you slander a dead man, you are a coward. Because you think the public will accept inventions from such as you, you are a fool."

Wright responded with a libel action of his own. However, the defence counsel for the Gladstones demolished the evidence presented by Wright and the jury not only found for the defendants, but also added the rider "In our unanimous opinion, the evidence that has been placed before us has completely vindicated the high moral character of the late Mr W E Gladstone." With Captain Wright having to pay £5,000 costs, the non-indictable libel had been very satisfactorily countered.

When one next passes John Batchelor's grave in Cathays Cemetery or his statue in the Hayes, remember how events after his death have influenced the law of libel.

John Batchelor headstone

Gordon Hindess

After the erection of the statue, the authorities had great difficulty in preventing it being vandalised. A special police guard was set up but this did not stop a William Thorn, a few months later, throwing yellow paint and coal tar over it. Thorn was a respectable man but his political leanings were rather strong. He was tried and found guilty, but gained the sympathy of the judge who required only that Thorn enter into a recognisance to pay £15 to a charity of his choice. He chose the Hamadryad Hospital Ship, the old man of war devoted to the care of seamen.

John Batchelor's grave, a double plot, can be found under the trees at the southern end of Section O, just across the way from the Cedar of Lebanon behind the chapels. The heavily inscribed red granite headstone includes details of many, but not all, family members. A transcription of the details appears on the next page.

The headstone shouts out "Plan ahead". The initial inscriptions enjoy generous space: the later ones are squashed in at the bottom, with the final line continued on the plinth. Unfortunately, the plinth, like the kerb, is in Radyr Stone, which is far from ideal for fine engraving and lacks the durability of granite: hence the incomplete transcription.

However, not all of the family are recorded here – there is no mention of the first two daughters and the second, third and fourth sons. Some of these must have died in infancy and are buried elsewhere, before Cathays Cemetery was opened. However, one, at least, lived to adulthood: Cyril Batchelor, with his brother Arthur Llewellyn, may be remembered locally as the founders, in 1880, of Penarth RFC, which was originally known as the Batchelor

XV. Cyril went on to operate as a metal merchant at Llanelli and Hartlepool and ended his days at Lapworth, near Solihull. The one non-Batchelor recorded on the headstone, William Edwards, was the husband of Edith Evangeline.

In memory of

JOHN BATCHELOR
BORN APRIL 10 1820 DIED MAY 29 1883
AND OF TOM EUSTACE HIS SON
DIED NOV 17 1862
AGED 2 YEARS
O REST IN THE LORD WAIT PATIENTLY FOR HIM AND
HE SHALL GIVE THEE THY HEARTS DESIRE
ALSO OF FANNY EDITH HIS WIFE
DIED MARCH 12 1909
AGED 85 YEARS
HER CHILDREN RISE UP AND CALL HER BLESSED
ALSO OF JOHN GEORGE HERBERT HIS ELDEST SON
BORN JULY 8 1854 DIED NOVEMBER 24 1912
ALSO OF ARTHUR LLEWELLYN, HIS FIFTH SON
WHO DIED NOVEMBER 19TH 1915 AND WAS BURIED IN THE
PROTESTANT CEMETERY VALPARAISO
ALSO OF ETHEL CAROLINE AGNES HIS FOURTH
DAUGHTER WHO DIED NOVEMBER 13TH 1916
ALSO OF EDITH EVANGELINE, HIS THIRD DAUGHTER
ALSO OF WILLIAM THOMAS EDWARDS M.D.L.L.D.
DIED JULY 7TH 1919
ALSO MARY DAVEY MILDRED BATCHELOR, HIS YOUNGEST DAUGHTER
DIED .... AGED 72 YEARS

Gordon Hindess

CHAPTER THREE

Dr Henry Paine (1817-1894)

Memorial to Henry Paine and his family

Gordon Hindess

Upon entering section L on the higher path from the chapels, and taking the grassy path, which arcs around to the right, the memorial to Dr Henry James Paine is just over half way round on the right.

The inscription on the red granite obelisk says that Henry James Paine died in 1894, at the age of 76 and that his widow, Eliza, died in 1904, aged 92. However, the rest of the story is more tragic. Their first three children are buried in St John's churchyard, Cardiff, since their deaths pre-date the opening of Cathays Cemetery, and died at the ages of 19 days, 4 months and 2 years 7 months in the years 1848 and 1849. It is probably not irrelevant that Cardiff suffered its worst cholera epidemic in 1849. Although their other two children reached adulthood, both died relatively young and failed to outlive their parents: their second daughter, Emily Louisa, died in 1884, aged 34, while their third son, Francis Trevor died in 1878, aged 25.

In the face of such personal tragedy, it is perhaps even more commendable that Henry James Paine should have done so much for the health and well-being of the people of Cardiff during his own lifetime.

In February 1866, the Mayor of Cardiff convened a meeting to discuss an extension to the Glamorgan & Monmouth Infirmary and Dispensary to accommodate new wards for patients with infectious diseases and ill seamen. It came as a surprise to the meeting to hear that Dr Paine, who was the local Medical Officer of Health, had already negotiated the loan of HMS Hamadryad from the Admiralty. Dr Paine believed the most suitable accommodation for seamen who were unwell was a ship.

HMS Hamadryad was the third ship of that name: the first was a 36-gun Spanish frigate, the Ninfa, which was acquired as a prize after grounding near Cape Trafalgar, purchased by the Admiralty for use as an armed transport, but it eventually sank close to Algiers. The second was another captured Spanish frigate, the Matilda, which remained in active service until 1813, when she was sold for £2,610.

The third Hamadryad was a 46-gun man-of-war, built at Pembroke Dock between 1819 and 1823 for £24,683, which never saw active service. It was laid up at Devonport until 1866, when orders were given for it to be broken up. Two other redundant warships had been brought to Cardiff in 1860, one to become the 'Ragged School' for homeless children, the other being used as a church for the Missions to Seamen. It has been suggested that this gave the idea of a Hospital Ship to Dr Paine.

The scheme was not universally supported. The Cardiff Times feared that the plan would fail ... but urged that the "very doubtful experiment" be implemented quickly, so that it would be fairly tested to enable a decision on the extension to the Infirmary, which had been postponed, to be made as soon as possible. The paper was less than complimentary about Dr Paine's judgement and commitment to the medical needs. The Cardiff & Merthyr Guardian was

The hospital ship, Hamadryad, moored in Cardiff Docks

Courtesy of Cardiff Central Library Local Studies Section

more supportive, being particularly concerned that the diseases of the world were not dragged through the streets of the town and allowed to fester in the middle of it. It also thought that there would "be more chances of an old or young salt's cure, floating in this hollow oak, with old mess mates about him, and the Union Jack wavering o'er him, than there would be in the most perfectly fitted ward in any infirmary."

In the event, Dr Paine's proposal was accepted and, only a month after the order to break up the ship, arrangements were in place for its conversion into a seamen's hospital ship for use in the Port of Cardiff. It was fitted out at a cost of £1,414 to receive between 60 and 65 inpatients, with facilities for a doctor, his medical staff, a matron and her nursing staff. On arrival in Cardiff, the ship was grounded on wasteland known as Rat Island, the area that subsequently grew into Tiger Bay.

Over 30 years, 173,000 patients from all over the world were treated on the ship. This included 1,285 with fractures or dislocations, 1,384 with wounds, and 2,098 with chest infections. Of the 1,182 fever cases, many came from the town itself. It was one of only two hospitals devoted to the free treatment of seamen of all nations, the other being the Dreadnought Seamen's Hospital, in Greenwich.

At a meeting to discuss the best means of celebrating the Diamond Jubilee of Queen

Victoria it was suggested that a permanent seamen's hospital should be built. This was opened on 29th June 1905 and as the Royal Hamadryad Seamen's Hospital continued to provide free medical treatment for seamen until 1948, when it was incorporated into the National Health Service. On becoming redundant, the hospital ship was taken to Bideford and broken up, although the

One of the hospital ship wards on the Hamadryad
Courtesy of Cardiff Central Library Local Studies Section

ship's bell and figurehead were preserved and kept initially in the new hospital. Today, the figurehead is one of the largest exhibits in the Cardiff Story Museum.

The growth of Cardiff in the 19th century was frantic. Between 1831 and 1856, the population grew from around 6,000 to over 30,000. The docks became very busy and prosperous as trade increased, aided by new railways and improvements to the Glamorgan Canal. But there was insufficient housing, resulting in overcrowding, poverty and poor sanitation. The Glamorgan Canal also served as a source for drinking water ... and for sewage disposal! Landore Court in St Mary Street illustrates the degree of overcrowding – in 1848, there were 27 two-roomed houses accommodating 500 people. Further, in 1858, Dr Paine who was by then Medical Officer of Health for Cardiff provided a list of 222 dwellings housing 2,920 people, including one house with 26 inhabitants.

The ship's figurehead in the Cardiff Story Museum
Paul Jones

Not surprisingly, disease was common and Cardiff suffered repeated epidemics, the spread of which was also aided by the increased movement of people, which came with growing trade. In 1842, the first cholera epidemic of the century struck Cardiff, killing many people.

The 1846/7 epidemic of typhus killed nearly 200 people, while cholera returned in 1849 and 1854, killing in excess of 365 and 200 people, respectively. In 1857, 150 deaths resulted from a smallpox infection in the area around Caroline Street. The fact that a cholera outbreak in 1866 only resulted in 76 deaths was seen as a measure of the success of measures that had been taken to improve health and sanitation.

In 1847, the Rammell Inquiry stated that Cardiff had dangerously polluted water and no sanitation, while the Public Health Act of 1848 permitted the establishment of local Boards of Health and the new position of Medical Officer of Health. It was an enabling, not a compulsory, act and implementation depended on the initiative of local communities, but Cardiff was among the first in Wales to grasp the opportunity offered by the new legislation.

Shortly afterwards, Dr Paine was appointed as Medical Officer of Health. The Cardiff Waterworks Company was set up to supply wholesome drinking water from clean sources and the 1850 Cardiff Waterworks Act granted the powers to do this. By 1856, a new system of sewerage/drainage was nearing completion, at a cost of £200,000.

Perhaps more important was a better understanding of the causes of diseases and the best way to control and minimise their spread. It had been commonly thought that epidemics had been caused by smells, bad food, cold and damp or, even, the "shocking habits of the Irish"! The Irish Potato Famine had resulted in a lot of immigrants in the years 1845 - 1852 and there was undoubtedly some anti-Irish sentiment at the time.

Under Dr Paine, Cardiff was divided into districts and a medical officer appointed for each district. At the

Dr Henry James Paine
Courtesy of Cardiff Central Library Local Studies Section

first sign of disease, every house would be visited once a day by a doctor. Houses were whitewashed with lime. People living near the canal were advised to move. Efforts were made to tackle the worst areas of overcrowding, which had the highest mortality rates. Flat Holm was acquired for the reception of immigrants with cholera so that the disease did not enter the town.

It was widely recognised that the improvements achieved were largely due to the efforts of Henry Paine, who was the Medical Officer of Health from 1853 to 1887. He often had to fight both medical and political opposition but, through his pioneering ideas to improve sanitation and keep Cardiff free from disease, it is estimated that he may have saved over 15,000 lives by the time of his retirement.

As if his medical role was not enough, Dr Paine also served as a Justice of the Peace for Cardiff, a role that was time-consuming and surprisingly diverse. As an example, he sat on the inquiry, in January 1886, into the circumstances attending the loss of the pilot cutter Gertrude through collision with the steamship Eliza Hunting, in Penarth Roads, the previous month. The Court found that the Eliza Hunting failed to keep a proper lookout. Its master was deemed guilty of neglect and had his certificate suspended for 3 months - a seemingly mild punishment in the circumstances.

Gordon Hindess

CHAPTER FOUR

Monuments

*A typical Gothic-style gravestone with a pointed arch,
labelled with common Victorian features*

Paul Jones

The memorials in a modern burial ground tend to be relatively small and similar in style. This is a result of more conservative rules, reflecting safety, maintenance and conformity considerations, a desire to limit the cost and today's view of what is tasteful. However, the Victorians, or at least the better off ones, were not so constrained so that memorials come in all shapes and sizes in Cathays Cemetery.

For anyone wishing to study memorial styles and classification, the Cemetery provides a wonderful opportunity. Therefore, this chapter presents a few types from the bewildering selection on display. To begin, the adjacent picture of a headstone is annotated to show the key features to look for on a Gothic-style gravestone. While this style might be relatively common in the period, the individual stonemason's artistry, complying with a family's wishes, shines out in the detail, which may be unique.

Starting with memorials that are generally quite low and typically longer than they are high, we have:

*1 **Ledger** – a flat slab set at ground level.*

*2 **Coped Stone or Hip Tomb** – since the ledger may be prone to wear (from being walked on), or be easily obscured by vegetation, autumn leaves or soil, it is logical to raise the slab and then bevel the sides to make the inscription easier to read from the side.*

*3 **Coped Stone: Cruciform (1894)** – a variation that probably reflects a stronger religious connotation.*

*4 **Coped Stone: Double Gabled (1877)** – a more elaborate variation.*

*5 **Chest Tomb (1865)** – looking like a stone coffin or sarcophagus, a design that can be traced back for thousands of years.*

*6 **Table Tomb (1923)** – may be regarded as a much more elaborate or intricately designed version of the chest tomb.*

Moving on to the upright memorials, there is a wide variety of those that typically stand up to no more than head height.

7 Grave Marker *– the smallest form of memorial in a durable material, in this case decorated with a cherub, but many carry no more than a brief inscription.*

8 Victorian Angel *– usually supported on a cross, as in this case. There are, of course, plain crosses or ones embellished with other carvings: for example, anchors are popular among the seafarers in Cathays.*

9 Triangular Headed, with Rustic Log Surround (1915) *– bringing nature into memorials has been a common theme over the years.*

10 Rustic Cross on a Pile of Rocks *– while there are obvious religious connotations, rocks represent permanence, stability, reliability and strength in almost all cultures.*

11 Scroll Memorial (1894) *– these seem to come in a bewildering range of styles.*

12 Art Nouveau (1908) *– appears on the scene towards the end of the nineteenth century.*

Finally, we look at a selection of those memorials that are usually the first to catch the eye, because of their dominating height.

13 Obelisk (1867) – *the most common example of the influence of Egyptian architectural style and particularly popular around hundred years ago.*

14 Pedestal Tomb: Classical (1922) – *choice of stone, decoration and size, provides ample scope for individualisation.*

15 Pedestal Tomb with Urn (1918) – *today, the urn is associated with cremation, but it is most popular from a time when cremation was uncommon. The urn is often draped with a cloth, symbolic of reverential access from earth to heaven. As an alternative, a sphere may top the pedestal.*

16 Gothic Revival Pedestal Monument – *a style that was particularly popular in Victorian times, and not just for buildings.*

17 Broken Column (1892) – *the pedestal may continue upwards with a column and sometimes this is broken, symbolic of a life cut short.*

18 Celtic Cross (1879) – *not surprisingly, popular in Wales. It is worth looking closely at the decorative patterning, which is often quite individualistic.*

The dates in brackets after the style refers to the date recorded as the first burial on the memorial.

Paul Jones provided the images of the memorials all of which can be found in Cathays Cemetery.

CHAPTER FIVE

The Price of Coal

*The Welsh National Mining Memorial near Nant-y-Parc primary school, Senghenydd
- centrepiece sculpture*

Gordon Hindess

The Senghenydd Mining Disaster of 1913

Senghenydd is a village just 12 miles to the north of Cardiff in South Wales. In the early 20th century, it was the location of The Universal Colliery and is ever more linked to the date of 14th October 1913.

From the first hours of the morning men and boys had been getting themselves prepared for the walk from their homes in the village and from nearby Abertridwr to the pithead. Fathers and sons together assembled waiting to be ushered into the cages to take them far below ground. Some were boys 14 years of age; others were there for the first time and just out of school. By 7am, all 950 workers had been lowered to the coal seams below and many had commenced work at the coalface. The banksman and the winders had started bringing up coal and lowering empty trams and supplies for the workers underground.

At 8 o'clock, the gyration of the wheels on the winding gear was normal and it seemed to the manager that it would be another uneventful day but ten minutes later whilst he was talking with the lamp room man there came a mighty explosion so loud that it was heard in Cardiff. There was the scream and clash of rending metal and the clang of falling debris. Clouds of dust and smoke were rising from the shaft.

Neither siren nor whistle was needed to alert the villagers. Within minutes, throngs of families, friends and neighbours were gathered fearing the worst yet hoping for the best.

The explosion was probably started by firedamp (methane) being ignited by sparking from electric bell signalling gear or from the accidental breakage of a Davy lamp. The initial explosion would have disturbed coal dust on the floor, raising a cloud that then also ignited. The shock wave ahead of the explosion would have raised yet more dust, so that the explosion was effectively self-fuelling. Miners not killed immediately by the fire and explosion would have died quickly from afterdamp, the gases formed by combustion, including carbon monoxide.

On that morning, nearly 950 men were working below ground. Production was undertaken from two shafts, the Lancaster and the York. Physically, the two shafts were quite close together, with York servicing the east side of the workings and Lancaster the west (obviously, whoever determined the names had a sense of both history and geographic relativity). However, the underground roadways were linked so that the two shafts provided circulating ventilation: York was the upcast (extracting foul air) and Lancaster the downcast (fresh air drawn in).

The explosion started in the west side workings where, in another historical quirk, the active districts were named Ladysmith, Pretoria, Kimberley and Mafeking, to commemorate the Boer Wars. The blast whipped through the west side passages but, somewhat miraculously, diverted up the Lancaster shaft, dramatically reversing the normal air flow here, driving the cage out of the top of the shaft and destroying the housing at the top. However, this saved over 500 miners in the east side, many of whom were unaware initially that anything was amiss and who only appreciated the magnitude of the tragedy after they had been evacuated via the York shaft. This remained operational despite the fact that fire raged a few hundred metres away, preventing rescue access into the stricken west side.

The explosion killed 439 miners and the following day one of the rescuers died.

Original Senghenydd Mine Disaster Memorial by entrance to Nant-y-Parc School. The simplified replica pithead winding gear is about 15 feet high.

Gordon Hindess

This was not the first disaster at the Universal Mine - twelve years earlier, on Friday 24th May 1901, an explosion had killed about 80 men and there had been but one survivor pulled from the mineshaft. The death toll would have been higher had the explosion not occurred at the end of a shift when most of the miners had been brought to the surface.

The managers and owners of the Universal were prosecuted after the second tragedy. It was found that recommendations aimed at improving safety; made following the 1901 disaster and new safety legislation laid down in the 1911 Coal Mines Act had not been fully implemented. Conditions at the pit had in fact worsened as the increase in production after 1901 had led to rising numbers of workers operating in confined spaces. Evidence showed that the Senghenydd pit was dangerously dry, dusty and gassy but, despite this, production there continued to expand. The manager was fined £24 resulting in the headline "Miners' Lives at 1s 1½d" while, only after an appeal, the owners also were fined £10 with costs of £5 5s.

William Hyatt, a miner who survived the explosion, commented: "My father always said there was more fuss if a horse was killed underground than if a man was killed. Men came cheap - they had to buy horses".

Amazingly, Universal Colliery was producing coal again by the end of November 1913 and full production was achieved by 1916. This was, of course, encouraged by World War One and the unprecedented demand for Welsh steam coal, most of it being used to fuel the battleships of the Royal Navy. The owners, Lewis-Merthyr Consolidated Collieries (whose Chairman was Lord Merthyr) prospered. However, the boom was not to last much longer - workmen and staff were given just one-day's notice of closure in March 1928. However, Powell Duffryn acquired the site in order to give extra ventilation to their Windsor Colliery at Abertridwr and later to the Nantgarw Colliery, so the Senghenydd shaft was only finally filled in 1979.

At the beginning of 1891, Senghenydd did not exist as a village - the Aber Valley was almost completely rural. However, later that year, a row of one-storey corrugated iron huts was erected to house the shaft sinkers and railway construction workers. These temporary buildings, known as "The Huts," seem to have been still housing families until at least 1914. The lack of housing closer to the mine explains why a number of employees resided in Cardiff and they would have travelled by workers' train each day.

Brass plaque on wooden cross recording the disaster

Gordon Hindess

The Cardiff victims were:-

David (aged 17) & Thomas (18) Jenkins of 23 Dalton Street

William Pain (34) of 63 Coburn Street

William Robson of 4 Minnie Street

Charles Peters (22) of 12 North Luton Place

George Pingree (25) of 30 Coburn Street

Frank Langmaid (17) of 44 Helen Street

Thomas Collier (45) of 19 Sophia Street

Samuel Manfield (16) of 45 Planet Street

William Jenkins (21) of 186 Cairn Street

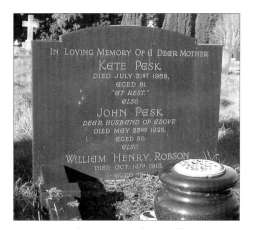

Headstone recording William
Robson's death

Gordon Hindess

The two young Jenkins boys, who had only been at the mine for a few months, share a grave in Section EF. Their coffins were carried through the streets to the cemetery nearby. William Pain and William Robson are in adjacent graves, while George Pingree is just a few plots away. George was newly married with a baby son, who died two months later and is buried with his dad.

Robson, a haulier in charge of a pit pony in the mine, was one of only two injured men brought out alive by rescuers on the day of the explosion, but he succumbed to his injuries on the way to King Edward VII Hospital (later to become Cardiff Royal Infirmary). Robson's is the only one of this cluster of graves with a headstone, but, at the request of the Friends of Cathays Cemetery, a wooden cross, with a plaque (as pictured on the previous page) commemorating the disaster, has been placed between the Jenkins and Pain graves, a few years ago. In the centenary year, the disaster was remembered in a special walk, which visited all the victims' graves. At this time, individual wooden crosses with plaques were placed at each unmarked grave.

Frank Langmaid is in an unmarked grave in Section EF. Thomas Collier and Samuel Manfield are in the older part of the Cemetery, in Sections R and S respectively. Only the last of these is marked by a headstone. There is no record in the burial records of William Jenkins or Charles Peters, but we have learned that the body of the latter was taken to his home village, Llantrithyd, where he was buried with his brother, John, another victim of the disaster.

In the village of Senghenydd, the original memorial to the disaster is outside the village's Nant-y-Parc Primary School, which is built on the site of the old mine. At St Cenydd School, Caerphilly stands a truck of coal and a list of the victims. The Senghenydd Salvation Army has a plaque remembering those they lost and a local public house has its own memorial.

Headstone recording Samuel Manfield's
death, with a reference to
Senghenydd colliery

Gordon Hindess

Thomas Jenkins

OED/AGE 27

12 Kingsley Place
Senghenydd

Noddwyd gan/Sponsored by
Jack & Marjorie Jenkins

David Jenkins

OED/AGE 17

23 Dalton Street
Cardiff

Noddwyd gan/Sponsored by
The Freemasons of
South Wales

William Jenkins

OED/AGE 21

186 Cairn Street
Cardiff

Noddwyd gan/Sponsored by
The Freemasons of
South Wales

Thomas E. Jenkins

OED/AGE 18

23 Dalton Street
Cardiff

Noddwyd gan/Sponsored by
Callum Hawkins

Tiles at the Nant-y-Parc memorial: three are for Cardiff miners buried in Cathays
Gordon Hindess

Walk of Remembrance at Nant-y-Parc
Gordon Hindess

Exactly one hundred years after the explosion a new memorial was dedicated at the site of the pit head, near the present Nant-y-Parc primary school.

The centrepiece, pictured at the start of this chapter, is a sculpture of a rescuer helping an injured miner. The rectangular wall around this is topped by 521 hand-made tiles, which were created in community workshops by local volunteers, including primary school pupils. Each tile records the name, age and address of one of the victims of the two disasters at Senghenydd, in 1901 and 1913.

Fundamental to raising the money for the memorial was a sponsorship plan for tiles, and the name of the sponsor is also included on them.

Conjoined with the rectangular wall is a circular Walk of Remembrance, bordered by tiles, which record every Welsh mining disaster, which claimed five or more lives.

These tiles are also hand-made and of similar style, but are much larger. Each records the colliery name, disaster dates (some had more than one qualifying disaster), number of fatalities, and the name of the sponsor of the tile. Poignantly, Aberfan is included in the memorial.

Aberfan tile beside the Walk of Remembrance

Gordon Hindess

Gordon Hindess

The Tynewydd Colliery Disaster of 1877

Great feats of heroism seem to go hand in hand with disasters. Often the first people into a mine after an explosion were the men's comrades and fellow workers. In 1877 such an event led to the presentation by Queen Victoria of four Albert Medals to the rescuers, the first ever awarded for gallantry on land. The Tynewydd disaster had additional repercussions. Rescue stations were formed around the country and inspectors began making routine inspections to prevent disasters instead of just determining a cause in the aftermath of catastrophe.

Late in the afternoon on April 11th 1877 at the Tynewydd coalmine northwest of Cardiff, near the head of the Rhondda Fawr valley, the day shift made their way to the pithead. Thomas Morgan and his two sons William and Richard started to make their way out when they were met by a sudden rush of air followed by a roar of water that knocked them back as it passed to a depth of their knees. Joining two others Edward Williams and William Cassia, they quickly made for the ventilation shaft only to find that it too was full of water.

They were now trapped in a higher section of the tunnels with water on both sides of them compressing the air. The water rose more slowly. The men sang hymns to keep up their morale as they banged the tunnel walls with stones to signal to any potential rescuers. They began to dig upwards to the passageway overhead. Meanwhile on the surface the roll call had been made and found to be 14 men short.

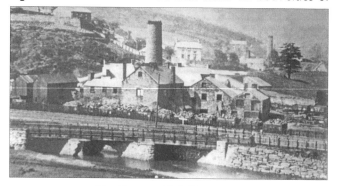

The Tynewydd Colliery 1877

On the surface men and relatives soon started to assemble to hear news of their comrades and loved-ones. The first men began to enter the mine and found the initial tunnels to be dry. As they pressed ahead, they listened for the noise of any survivors. They heard the singing of hymns but over 36 feet of coal separated them from the trapped men. The rescuers worked in four-man shifts - two to dig, two to remove rock. By the next morning, the rescuers could hear the voices of the trapped men, and telling them to stay well back, began to remove the final few feet of rock. Here the first tragedy happened. One trapped man eager to gain his freedom stood too near the excavated hole. When the connection was made, compressed air forced debris out of the hole onto the rescuers and the trapped man's head was sucked into the breach killing him instantly. The dead man's father had to pull the body back in order to enlarge the hole to enable their escape.

Elsewhere that night, escaping air had alerted a crew to another trapped man's signals below. The rescuers sank another shaft only to find the cavity full of water and a miner and his 13-year old butty drowned as the escaping air had allowed the water to rise.

It seemed that the source of the flooding had been from a nearby abandoned mine. Officials seemingly ignored warnings of digging the current mine tunnels too close, leading to water seepage. Pumps were hurried in to remove the water, but it would take too long to pump out to save the other miners. Divers were brought in all the way from London but failed to reach the men.

At this time, in the early days of mining in these valleys, many of the miners could only speak Welsh, so a translator was required to speak to the English press reporters who had assembled on hearing news of the disaster.

The remaining men below ground had managed to reach a work-face where they had laid on ledges above the water wedging themselves into a coal tram, huddling together to keep warm. One problem was that they were 113 feet away from their rescuers and could be drowned in the inrush of water when the breach was made. They might also starve if the operation took too long. Each man on the Rescue team had been warned of the dangers from the water, the gas, and the compressed air but many still volunteered for the role.

Officials had meanwhile determined that the use of airlocks would solve the problem of compressed air release upon breach.

Eventually voices were heard through the rock, and small holes were bored through so that food might be passed in. Engineers prepared the first airlock but could not make it airtight. As volunteers bored another hole into the intervening coal, a large discharge of gas put out the flames in the safety lamps. There was a possibility of explosive gas being present and this played on the fears of every miner. However, Abraham Dodd, Thomas Jones, William Thomas, Isaac Pride, and Daniel Thomas continued digging. As the breach was made the water climbed up the trapped miners, coming to stop just short of their chins. Isaac Pride made a bridge with his body so Abby Dodd could pass the men over. One by one, the trapped men emerged from their would-be tomb. A jubilant crowd welcomed them on the surface. All the rescued men would "suffer from the bends", the condition associated with deep-sea divers who come to the surface too quickly, but they all recovered.

Although only five men lost their lives at Tynewydd, in 1877 alone 160 men would perish in the South Wales Coalfields. On average 1,000 deaths occurred every year in the early 1900s. The men at Tynewydd had suffered 10 days trapped underground. It was an incredible feat of courage by the men, who kept digging beyond their endurance in the face of great danger.

Cathays Cemetery's link to the disaster is that one of the men who broke through to the trapped miners was the mine owner, Thomas Jones. He is buried in section L. He was tried for manslaughter in connection with the disaster, accused of failing to take precautions after earlier reports of water seepage, but was acquitted on the grounds that he believed a geological fault would have sealed off any chance of a leak from the old pit.

As a final note, one of the rescuers, Abraham Dodd was not among those cited for a medal, as he appears to have had some harsh words for the mine owners and management. At this time, criticizing those in authority was virtually unheard of.

We are indebted to britishheritage.com for the main details of this article.

Paul Jones

The monument to Thomas Jones

Paul Jones

CHAPTER SIX

Archibald Hood (1823-1902)

If one takes the drive from the chapels, through the centre of Section M, one will find the tallest obelisk in the Cemetery, about 10 metres off to the right. It is distinctive not just because of its size: it is also made from particularly attractive fine-grained grey granite. The inscription on it will tell us that this is the memorial to Archibald Hood and some of his family.

The memorial was erected on the death of his wife, Cochrina Walker (Walker was her maiden surname) on 27th March 1891, at the age of 65.

The Hood obelisk

Gordon Hindess

Hood rose, largely through his own endeavour, from humble beginnings in Ayrshire to become a wealthy and respected engineer and businessman, who exhibited a social conscience that set an example for his age. Early in his working life, he became friendly with William Walker, a coal pioneer in South Ayrshire, eventually marrying his eldest daughter Cochrina. They had four sons and a daughter, who we look at below.

Commemorated on the obelisk is Robert Raeburn Hood who was born in Tradeston, Glasgow, on 20th June 1856. His primary education was at Rosewell, in Midlothian, and he then went to Clifton College, Bristol. It is thought that he studied Mining Engineering at Edinburgh University. He became manager of the Gilfach Goch Colliery and then represented the Glamorgan Coal Company's interests overseas, including South America. It was while carrying out these duties that he died on 4th December 1915, in Santiago, Chile, where he is buried.

William Walker Hood was born in Rosewell, on 6th September 1857, and educated at the local school, then Clifton College. He studied Mining Engineering on the Continent and became General Manager of the Glamorgan Coal Company's collieries in the Rhondda Valley. His home was Hen Glyncornel, Llwynypia, where he played a prominent part in the life of the Valley. Hen Glyncornel is still there, but reincarnated as a nursing home. William made a special study of mining rescue methods and established a reputation for his fearlessness and devotion in rescue work, during which he had a number of hairbreadth escapes. William and his father were the first to use the watering of coal dust to reduce the risk of gas explosions. He played a prominent part in the establishment of the School of Mines at Treforest and continued to take a special interest in it.

On the death of his maternal grandfather, William Walker, he inherited Ballochmyle Colliery in Ayrshire and worked this until the seams were exhausted. On the death of his father, in 1902, he became Managing Director of the Glamorgan Coal Company until the Cambrian Coal Company bought it out in 1908. He also held a directorship of the Lothian Coal Company and was Vice-Chairman of the Barry Railway Company.

Latterly he had his home at Tredean, a country mansion near Devauden, and also owned Invergeldie at Glenlednock in Scotland. During the last years of his life, he was engaged in experiments in the use of electricity in agriculture but these were never completed because on 23rd March 1923, while travelling home by train from London, he inadvertently opened the carriage door, fell and was killed instantly. He was buried with his parents in Cathays Cemetery. He was unmarried.

The formative years of James Archibald Hood, born in 1859, mirrored that of his elder brothers but, after Clifton College, he also had some education in Paris, at a mining school in Mons, Belgium, and in Germany, as well as at Edinburgh University.

Unlike his elder brothers, he did marry (though relatively late in life), in 1903. His wife, Violet was the daughter of Matthew Montgomerie Bell, an Edinburgh J.P. They lived in the Hood family house in Rosewell where they had five daughters. Though one of these died in childhood, the others all married and had children, so the line continues, though not with the Hood name. One of the daughters, Jean, married Sir Philip Dundas, 4th Baronet of Arniston, in Midlothian, while the youngest, Celia, ended her days, as Mrs Noel Baskett in Auckland, New Zealand. On the death of his brother William, James inherited his country house, Tredean.

James Archibald Hood was General Manager of his father's collieries in and around Rosewell and, on their amalgamation with those of Lord Lothian to form the Lothian Coal Company; he became its first General Manager. On the death of his father, he became Managing Director, and in 1911 Chairman and Managing Director. In 1924, he gifted Heriot-Watt College (now incorporated in Edinburgh University) £15,000 to found the Hood Chair of Mining. He was created an Honorary LLD of the College in 1928 and, at various times, held numerous directorships in industries as diverse as papermaking, electric power and motor vehicles.

James Archibald Hood died in 1941 at his home, Midfield House, Lasswade, and was buried in Hawthornden Cemetery, Rosewell, joining his wife and the daughter who died in childhood. He is not mentioned on the obelisk in Cathays Cemetery.

The education of Archibald Hood, born on 4th May 1861, followed that of his brothers but, after Clifton College, he studied medicine and went on to become a general practitioner in Bridgend. He married Constance Edwards and they had two children. Their son, Frederick was ordained and went on to become the Principal of Pusey House (the Anglican Centre in

Oxford) and Canon Chancellor of St Paul's Cathedral. Their daughter, Constance, married and became Mrs Molyneaux. Archibald died as a result of a riding accident at Laleston and was buried in Nolton churchyard, but he too is remembered in Cathays Cemetery, on the Hood memorial.

Eliza Agnes Walker Hood (Ella) was born on 7th January 1864, also in Rosewell, and went to the local primary school. She married Mr Walter Shirley and they had two sons and three daughters. One son died at school age, and the other was killed in the First World War. On the death of her father, Mrs Shirley became a Director of the Lothian Coal Company, and at that time resided at The Woodlands, at the top of Leckwith Hill (locals may remember this large property in its more recent guise as a nursing home). Their youngest daughter, Beryl, became Mrs Heard and her daughter, Jacqueline, married Dr Arthur Conner Lysaght. Arthur was the second son of D. C. Lysaght, of the steel firm of that name, operating at the Orb Steelworks, Newport. We have followed the Hood line down through four generations in this case, because it shows a continuing connection to Cardiff. Arthur was a senior surgeon to the United Cardiff Hospitals and died in 1963 at Cardiff Royal Infirmary, the hospital he had served faithfully for thirty years.

While it is not unlikely that Archibald Hood hoped that his legacy would include the continuance of the family name, it is implicit in the story of his children why there is no evidence of that today. However, what of the man himself?

Archibald Hood was born in Kilmarnock, Ayrshire, on the 4th June 1823, the eldest son of Robert Hood, an overman at a Kilmarnock colliery. His mother died when he was a child and, within the limited means of his father, he had only a basic education. He began work in the same colliery as his father and, at the age of 13, was in charge of a surface engine and working at least 12 hours a day.

However, with his own desire to improve himself and his father's support, his limited spare time was spent extending his knowledge, particularly in mining and geology. When he was twenty, his father was appointed manager of a colliery near Glasgow. The proximity of higher education facilities here allowed Archibald to go to evening classes, at which he evidently excelled. It was only two years later that, as a qualified mining engineer, he was appointed Chief Mineral Agent and Engineer to Messrs Dunlop & Wilson, Ironmasters, and, in this capacity, he planned and managed the development of a large area in South Ayrshire for coal and ironstone mining. It was at this time that he became friendly with William Walker, whose eldest daughter, Cochrina, he was to marry.

However, he saw that profit lay not only in winning the basic minerals, but also in the associated service industries. This was to lead to him developing interests in brick and tile works and railways.

After a few years, he became a partner in Bankhead Colliery near Glasgow, but disposed of this interest in 1856 when he became involved in the Lothian coalfield by taking a lease on Whitehill Colliery at Rosewell and making his home at Rosedale House in the village. Mining had taken place in the area for at least a century, but the pits were quite shallow, with ladder access and simple hoisting gear to remove the coal and to provide worker access. Hood brought more professional and dynamic management to Whitehill and to smaller adjoining collieries at Skelty Muir, Gorton, Eldin, Carrington and Polton, which he later acquired. In 1866, Hood described Whitehill as being about 50 or 60 fathoms (3/400 feet) deep and ventilated by furnace. In 1878, a new Whitehill Mine winding shaft was sunk and this remained in operation throughout the early 20th century.

One of the major problems at Rosewell was the transportation of coal and other products to surrounding markets, by horse and cart over roads of poor quality. Appreciating that movement of his products by rail was vital, he applied himself to the development of the Polton and Penicuik railways, which were not only beneficial to his own interests, but also to the local paper mills. Following this, the family maintained a connection with the paper mills until at least the 1940s.

It was around this time that Hood realised that an amalgamation with the adjacent collieries owned by Lord Lothian would be of mutual benefit. However, it was not until 1890 that he finally attained this goal, when his Whitehill interests merged with those of the Marquess of Lothian at Newbattle to form the Lothian Coal Company Ltd. with a share capital of £500,000. The main shareholders were the Marquess and Hood: they became Chairman and Managing Director respectively with Archibald becoming Chairman on the death of the Marquess in 1900. The merger was to create one of the most successful mining concerns in the country. The new company leased 22 square miles of coalfield, owned 600 wagons and locomotives, 700 cottages, and Whitehill Brick and Tile Works.

The Marquess' pits were working the eastern side of the Midlothian coalfield, which, like the South Wales coalfield, is dish-shaped. There was a need to work the coal at the deeper levels of the dish and a large level area to the south of the village of Newtongrange was identified as a site for a new colliery. This site was alongside the Edinburgh to Hawick railway line, which provided a ready route for transporting coal. This line closed in the Beeching cuts, in the late 1960's, but readers may recognise this as the route that was resurrected in 2015 as the Borders Railway.

The sinking of the new deep mine, the Lady Victoria Colliery, named after the Marquess's wife, started in 1890. The colliery, one of the deepest in the country and using the most modern equipment then available, became the jewel of the company's crown for 60 years. With a work force of 1,200 men, it was the main employer for the village of Newtongrange. Many regard it as the first "super pit". The colliery lasted for 91 years (in the later period being under the control of the National Coal Board) and over its life produced nearly 40 million tons of coal, a Scottish record.

Before leaving Scotland, we should point out that, if there is a visible Hood legacy today, it is in the area of the Midlothian collieries and mining villages, which are about 10 miles to the south-east of the centre of Edinburgh, just outside the ring road (A720) and adjacent to the A7.

Rosedale House, where most of Hood's family were born, is a listed building and remains as a private house on the southern outskirts of the village of Rosewell, where the Rosewell Tavern is also located. This is the original cooperative building, which Hood established. At Bonnyrigg, there is an estate in which all streets use the name Sherwood, the name of Hood's Cardiff mansion. Midfield House, Lasswade, which was the home of James Archibald, is a listed Georgian Manor. It remains an impressive building, even though it has been converted into maisonettes: these currently sell at £200,000 for a modest two-bedroomed apartment.

The Whitehill Colliery site has been reclaimed as a woodland park, while the Lady Victoria Colliery is now the Scottish Mining Museum. It is not quite the same as Big Pit, at Blaenavon, as only the above ground buildings are used, the underground workings having been sealed off when the pit closed. Next door, the Victorian mining village of Newtongrange is well preserved. The single storey terraced houses, built of bricks produced in Hood's brickworks, form a geometric pattern of streets, called simply First Avenue to Tenth Avenue, in a compact L-shape, enclosing the spacious Welfare Park. This estate does not have the run-down look of much of the old housing stock in some Welsh mining communities – a testament to the quality of the original construction and the benevolence of the employer who provided the houses.

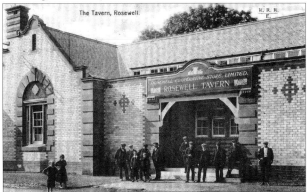

Rosewell Tavern

Courtesy of Midlothian Council Local History Library

This already seems like an impressive achievement in the life of one man, but we have not touched on the Welsh part of the story!

At the same time as he was consolidating his interests in Lothian, Hood was turning his mind to the potential opportunities in South Wales. The special qualities of South Wales steam coal had been brought into prominence during the Crimean War, being used for the first time by the Royal Navy. Welsh steam coal combined high calorific value with the ability to generate heat quickly, making possible rapid generation of steam. It had the added attraction of minimising smoke emission, making naval vessels less obvious at sea. Subsequently, the Rhondda Valley was to produce more steam coal than any other South Wales valley. In Glamorgan, annual outputs were to rise from nearly 6 million tons in 1860 to around 35 million tons in 1911.

Demand for this coal had been increasing at a dramatic rate, and the fact had not gone unnoticed by some Scottish commercial interests. In 1860, Hood was commissioned on an expenses paid basis by two Liverpool based Scots, Archibald Campbell and Gilbert Mitchell-Innes, to visit South Wales and assess the potential. His specific task was to look at Wern Colliery, Llantrisant, which had been newly purchased by the Liverpool partnership. He quickly established that the colliery was not going to meet their long-term expectations, and he then took time out to look at other mining possibilities, particularly in the Rhondda Valley, which, at the time, had few mines, and those were mainly at the lower end of the Valley.

Hood joined Campbell and Mitchell-Innes in the Ely Valley Coal Company Partnership and by 1862 had taken over management of the Welsh operations. He immediately turned his attention to the area around Llwynypia, at the time, a pastoral idyll with a grove of trees, presumably favoured by magpies, as the Welsh name implies. Boring operations started in July 1862 with satisfactory results although, some years later, it was discovered that there was a gap in the upper seam just west of the trial bore. Had the bore been sunk at this point, the course of Hood's life might have been very different! Shaft sinking at the new Glamorgan Colliery started in March 1863 and, despite serious difficulties with water and running sand, coal was reached in the Rhondda No 2 seam in March 1864. The Rhondda No 3 seam was reached ten months later.

Most evidence of Llwynypia Colliery has disappeared under new roads and a superstore, but the large engine house, built in 1905, remains and is a Grade II Listed building. Today, the engine house, built of yellow and red brick with stone and concrete dressings under a Welsh slate roof, has a neglected appearance, sealed off and hidden by ivy. Listing is not of itself a guarantee of preservation.

In 1863, Hood started mining at Gilfach Goch, where the colliery was known locally as the "Scotch Pit", and the company name was changed to Glamorgan Coal Company, which was to go on to operate six pits and become one of the top six mine operators in South Wales. Even at this early stage, Hood had established practical control over the company's operations, with his partners becoming "sleepers". By the 1890s, the company's shareholding was virtually all held by the Hood family.

The output of the prized steam coal steadily increased. The coal was marketed under the name of "Hood's Merthyr" and became one of the best-known coals on the Admiralty list for well over 30 years and was used by foreign navies and leading steamship companies. At its peak, the Glamorgan Coal Company was to produce 1 million tons of coal per year and employ 3,500 men.

Sherwood House, Newport Road in the early 1930s

Cardiff Central Library Local Studies Section

With his Welsh interests outstripping those in Scotland, Hood moved initially to Gilfach House in Gilfach Goch then, in 1867, took up permanent residence with his family at Sherwood House, in Newport Road, Cardiff. This was one of a row of Gothic mansions, which gave way to offices about 60 years ago, and was next to the now disused St James' Church.

At about the same time, the Company's head office was moved from Llwynypia to 6 Bute Crescent, Cardiff, adjacent to the docks.

Two by-products of coal mining, fire clay and small coal, were produced in great quantities, but Hood put these to profitable use. He established one of the largest brickworks in South

Wales, producing 10,000 bricks per day from the fire clay. A second ancillary operation was the production of coke from waste coal. Eventually, he had 281 coke ovens at Llwynypia and Gilfach Goch, producing 1,400 tons of coke per week, marketed under the names of "Hood's Patented Coke" and "Glamorgan Foundry Coke", the latter name reflecting the demand from the iron and steel industry. The coke rapidly gained both home and international recognition. While no by-products were extracted in the coking process, the waste gases were used to generate steam.

Hood believed in taking advantage of, and in many cases being in the forefront of, the latest developments. Examples of this were his use of compressed-air engines and, more importantly, electricity in mines. His belief in electricity was later to have him appointed to the Government Commission on Electricity in Mines, and also to become the first Chairman of the South Wales Electric Power Distributing Company.

As his status in the commercial and general life of South Wales grew, so did the positions which he held over the years, including Justice of the Peace; President, Cardiff Chamber of Commerce; Chairman, Monmouthshire and South Wales Coal Owners Association; Chairman, South Wales Institute of Engineers; President, Mining Association of Great Britain; Chairman, Sliding Scale Joint Committee (a management and union wage negotiating body for the mining industry in South Wales); Member of the Government Commission on Mining Royalties. He also wrote a major mining paper on "The Explosive Nature of Coal Dust".

6 Bute Crescent today

Gordon Hindess

By the 1870s, such was the demand for South Wales coal that the existing Bute East and West Docks were incapable of coping with the tonnage. Ships were being delayed in loading, coal was held in railway wagons longer than necessary and coal masters in the Valleys had to reduce output or stock coal, both actions having a negative impact on their profits. Of course, the main shareholder in the Docks and the Taff Vale Railway was the Marquess of Bute. Although the Marquess had obtained an Act of Parliament to build a further

Archibald Hood JP

Cardiff Central Library Local Studies Section

dock at Cardiff, the start had been delayed. One of the reasons for this was a requirement for additional revenue from the coal freighters. Discussion between the parties was protracted and eventually escalated to the House of Commons. A group of the freighters, led by David Davies of Llandinam, another South Wales coal master with mines in the upper Rhondda, and Archibald Hood, decided that a new and independent dock should be built at Barry. They were joined by local landowner, Lord Windsor (later 1st Earl of Plymouth), who also owned Penarth Docks. Against tremendous resistance from the powerful Bute interests, they pushed through Parliament the Barry Docks and Railway Act, to which Hood was one of the signatories.

The Barry Dock and Railway cost about £2 million (perhaps £2 billion today) to build. At the opening ceremony on 18th July 1889, Hood, in toasting the counsel, solicitor and parliamentary agents, said that he would be very happy to work with them again ... but that one Barry Docks was quite enough in a lifetime. The Earl of Plymouth was Chairman of the new company with David Davies as his Deputy and Davies' statue stands outside the Dock Office to this day. Although Davies received most of the public credit, the engineering brain and most consistent supporter of the project was almost certainly Hood, and he did become Deputy Chairman on the death of Davies a few years later.

Barry Dock 1901
Courtesy of Glamorgan Archives

Surprisingly, there does not appear to have been any lasting acrimony with the Bute family and, in 1902, just a few months before his death, Hood presented an address to the young Marquess on his 21st birthday. Apparently, he spoke with such feeling on his connections with the family over the years, that the Marchioness was visibly moved.

We have seen what an exceptional engineer and businessman Archibald Hood was but there was much more to this remarkable man.

From the earliest days in Rosewell, Hood took a paternal interest in his workforce, creating a model village with each cottage having a garden. He was deeply involved in the life of the village: he became a benefactor for many of its activities and was Chairman of the Parish Council for a while. He was an Elder and Trustee at the Rosewell Parish Church and the Rev. John Hunter, who became Minister in the 1870s, was a lifelong friend.

Hood was concerned about workers getting into debt by buying "on-tick" from local traders, so encouraged the development of co-operatives. By acting as Treasurer initially, he ensured the security of the funds and correct accounting. He also introduced the "Gothenburg" system of public house, where profits from the sale of alcohol were ploughed back into the community, providing facilities like parks and libraries. He later encouraged the setting up of a similar system in Newtongrange, where he also ensured that decent houses with gardens were built for his workforce. As a result, Newtongrange became one of the best mining villages in the country.

Hood showed similar consideration for his workers in Wales, providing cottages with gardens, and erecting schools and institutes furnished with reading rooms. It was reported that Llwynypia was the only place where sports were encouraged by the colliery proprietor. In Gilfach Goch, a reading room was established for use by the workmen of the Glamorgan Coal Company and the first colliery school was established, in 1870. The Company was active in the supervision of the school and, around 1875, the Llantrisant School Board decided that there should be a schoolhouse and school for 309 pupils. Hood was closely involved in the discussions and, when the premises were built, his company paid one third of the cost.

He was probably astute enough to understand that men who spent much of their lives underground would appreciate decent homes and outdoor recreations such as gardening, which could also provide cheap vegetables for families. Of course, a more satisfied workforce worked better for the company.

Even in Wales, Hood maintained close control of his Scottish business interests and this relied on frequent reports and correspondence. However, these papers were not confined to business, as he would also enquire about social and welfare matters. A keen bowler himself, he encouraged

School house and school, Gilfach Goch

Gordon Hindess

the installation of bowling greens and, only six months before his death, he opened the Newbattle Bowling Green.

A staunch Presbyterian, Hood encouraged the establishment of churches in his company's communities and he was also involved in the Presbyterian Church in Cardiff. In Gilfach Goch, before a proper church was built, he gave permission for Welsh Baptists and Welsh Independents to use the carpenter's shop at the colliery for their Sunday service. In 1867, he subscribed £25 (say, £2,000 today) to assist in the installation of a clergyman in the community, but cautioned, "that the subscription should not be considered as necessarily forthcoming in future years if the venture proved unsuccessful".

He showed great loyalty to those who gained his respect and this appeared to be returned. An example of this can be found on a gravestone in Hawthornden Cemetery, Rosewell, which bears the inscription "Sacred to the Memory of Alex McGregor, Underground Manager at Rosewell who died 15th June 1891 in his 55th year and who was for 35 years the faithful servant of Archibald Hood by whom this memorial is erected". In South Wales too, it is recorded that Hood looked after many of his elderly employees.

He was the first President, and undoubtedly the "father" of the Cardiff Caledonian

Society, which was formed in 1886. Even with many local "leaders of industry" in its membership, Hood dominated its early operation, particularly in widening the Society's original social function to give a more charitable outlook. There were many Scots in the area and the charity assisted those who had fallen on hard times. The Society's records are a sad catalogue of social history, with families being left poverty-stricken on the death of the breadwinner, old people on their own, young men unable to work due to tuberculosis or other illness, children being left without parents and many other examples of distress. In these cases, the Society provided money, practical help or, even, paid for the individual or family to re-join their kin in Scotland.

The final act of charity was a proper burial - with names recorded on a stone - for men and women who otherwise would have been given a pauper's grave. Early in the 20th century, James Manuel, a JP and Manager of the London & Provincial Bank, Cardiff, left a legacy, which initially provided 18 grave spaces and the headstone to record the gift.

The Society remains a registered charitable trust to this day and as custodians of the Manuel Legacy. Over the years, four further graves were acquired in the New Cemetery. However, it seems that there remains space for a total of nine further interments, distributed across five graves, even though the last burial was in 1939! For the Society's centenary, in 1986, the main grave and stone were rebuilt, cleaned and repainted.

As with many such charities, needs change and they respond accordingly. Therefore, we learn that during the First World War they provided a welcome and comforts, such as hot drinks, sandwiches

Main Caledonian Society grave headstone
Gordon Hindess

and cigarettes, to the vast number of troops passing through Cardiff. In its early days, the Society helped in cases of real distress but, as these became fewer, other ways to assist were found, such as providing financial awards for educational purposes to carefully chosen Scottish students in Cardiff. There was a longstanding association between the Society and the Sir Gabriel Woods Mariners Home in Greenock and, from time to time, old mariners acceptable to the Home were sent back there for their retirement.

Another facet of Hood's character was his love of music. In the 1898 St Andrew's Night dinner, Madame Gwen Cosslett-Heller, a professional singer from London, sang "Coming Through The Rye" to an arrangement by Hood himself. He particularly appreciated Welsh choral music and he gave generous support to the local society at Llwynypia, as well as to the colliery band. In 1900, he presided over a musical evening arranged by the Rosewell Co-operative Society.

Archibald Hood died at Sherwood House on 27th October 1902, at the age of 79. Even up to the day before his death, he had been working on a new wages agreement aimed at solving a dispute in the South Wales mining industry.

Hood himself might have been most pleased by those tributes after his death from representatives of his workforce. Mr William Abraham, the leader of the South Wales Miners' Federation and Rhondda's first MP, said that he had been one of the best friends of the colliery workers, while another official of the Federation said that, "his quaint Scottish humour made a difficult task more pleasant than it might have been". Other tributes included " ... a good relationship existed between him and his workmen", "He never forsook old workmen." and " ... he had always taken interest in the social and intellectual welfare of his workmen and their families".

Hood statue at Llwynypia

Gordon Hindess

The large attendance at the funeral in Cathays Cemetery included 100 workmen from the Glamorgan Coal Company as well as representatives from Midlothian. The service was taken by his old friend from Rosewell, the Rev. John Hunter. Later, in Rosewell Parish Church, Rev. Hunter led a thanksgiving service, referring to Hood as a man of untiring industry, unswerving rectitude and fearless courage.

Hood may have missed out in having a statue at Barry Docks, but he does have a statue in Llwynypia, commissioned by a grateful workforce and community. It was unveiled three years after his death – by leading trade unionist and MP, William Abraham. The statue is unusual being coloured, with striking yellow trousers.

The rags-to-riches story of Archibald Hood was one of the most remarkable in the second half of the 19th century. He never forgot his Scottish origins and remained a straightforward man, who never actively sought publicity for himself.

A simplified Hood Family tree is provided in the Appendix.

A fuller account of Hood's life can be obtained in "From Rosewell to the Rhondda, the story of Archibald Hood a great Scots mining engineer" by Archie Blyth (published in 1994). We are pleased to acknowledge the help derived from this book in producing this chapter.

Gordon Hindess

CHAPTER SEVEN

A Toiler's Life

Near the path junction, at the most northerly point of Section R is the memorial to James Mullin, his wife Annie and other family members. Luckily, for researchers, James Mullin wrote an autobiography - "The Story of a Toiler's Life" - during World War I, although it was not published until two years after his death (it was reprinted in 2000 by University College Dublin Press). Without this work, we would have struggled to do justice to the story of this remarkable man ... and would not have had a ready-made title for this chapter.

The Great Famine was in its early stages when James and Bridget Mullin's first child (also named James) was born in 1846. The working class family lived in a two roomed, thatched cottage in Cookstown, County Tyrone. When James senior died later the same year, Bridget and her son were left without any means of support. However, Bridget was a proud and resourceful woman, labouring in the fields in summer and spinning flax during the winter. Fortunately, she owned the cottage and was able to augment her income by letting one of the rooms to a family and the pigsty in the garden to another tenant. In the garden, she grew enough potatoes to tide them over the winter and, even in the worst of the famine, she never accepted the soup and meal relief that was distributed in the town.

Famine was followed by typhus, which spread easily where many families lived in one room, sometimes shared with animals such as pigs and chickens. There was no water-pump

The Mullin Memorial
Gordon Hindess

in Cookstown, so water was obtained either from a well in the garden or from a nearby stream. Mrs. Mullin, without any thought for the safety of herself and young James, had no qualms about helping the sick and dying in her neighbours' houses and in laying out corpses. Although only a young child at the time, James was never to forget the acrid stench that accompanied the fever.

James was taught to read by his mother and, initially, attended a local "school" in the kitchen/living room of the master. This arrangement ended with the sudden death of the teacher. Although Bridget was a strict Catholic, she allowed her son to attend the local Protestant school and subsequently between the ages of eight and eleven, he attended the National School. This latter was administered by Catholics but was co-educational and accepted children from all religions. By the time he had reached the most senior class, he was one of the best at reading and English comprehension and had developed a passion for books, which was to remain with him throughout his life.

However, at eleven, circumstances dictated that he leave school and start helping to support the family. He had acquired a reputation for scholarship that led to a demand from neighbours to write letters on their behalf, a commission that was often accompanied by a rare treat, a cup of tea and a slice of white bread. He also read at wakes, sitting as close as possible to the head of the corpse, with a solemnity that touched the hearts of the older women. His first casual job, weeding crops of flax, oats and potatoes, gleaning in the harvest fields and gathering potatoes in the autumn, earned sixpence a week. This back bending work for 10½ hours a day was only relieved when it rained … but then the pay also stopped! With the cheapest books on sale costing two shillings, the opportunity to indulge his passion was limited. Eventually, he gained permanent employment as a cowherd, earning three shillings a week, including Sundays and Christmas Day. After 2½ years of this, he was put in charge of the pigs and poultry but, on the very first day, he was caught reading by his master and given his notice.

An early riser, James was able to pursue his studies before he left for work in the morning and came to appreciate poetry. He submitted some patriotic verse of his own to The Irishman newspaper and its appearance in print encouraged him to produce more, leading to him winning the title of "Poet". Writing poetry was to stay with him as a recreation, but he never expected to achieve poetic distinction, even describing himself in the following terms:

> *Our author is rather a pert young prig.*
> *His wit is small as his conceit is big.*
> *He has the Devil's own amount of cheek,*
> *However, all he earns is three bob a week!*

James started an apprenticeship with a cartwright but, after a couple of years of overwork and negligible training, he left for a better paid job with a local timber merchant who also owned cart making and blacksmithing businesses. By the time, he was 18; he was a proficient wheel maker and found a new job at five shillings a week. He was to stay there for 4 years, with the wages, regularity of hours, and tempo of working being some compensation for suffering under a cruel master. While his circumstances were more comfortable, his health and strength were below average, due to under-nutrition, which, in his case, was made worse by a dislike of potatoes, the Irish staple. James continued to use what leisure time he had to improve his knowledge of literature, history and politics and he began to study the classics.

Mullin's intellectual ability had not passed unnoticed and he was invited to join a literary and scientific society that had recently formed in Cookstown. The membership consisted mainly of clerks, shopkeepers, schoolmasters and students; he was the only workman in the district to be accepted into that circle. To attend the weekly meetings, he had to sacrifice his lunch-hour in order to leave early to get to the meetings. He took an active part in the discussions and debates, and presented his own essays and poems to the society. One of the latter, entitled "Genius", was published by the Society and sold for sixpence a copy.

Around the same time, the Fenian Association was making great headway in Ireland. James had been indoctrinated into Republicanism by his mother and delighted in reading books and papers that glorified Irish independence. When the organisation spread to Cookstown, he was one of the first recruits to take the oath of allegiance. The local Fenians were an unlawful military body, secretly drilled by militiamen at night, but without arms or equipment. Their enemies were more the ecclesiastical authorities, rather than the government, and Mullin was one of the first Fenians in the district to attract the notice and incur the displeasure of the clergy. The local priest ordered him to sever his connection with the movement, but Mullin simply refused to obey. Although this served to reinforce the private doubts about religious matters that he harboured, his respect for his mother's deep devotion to the Catholic faith meant that he would not reveal his true attitude towards the Church. His mother's view of his association with the organisation was one of friendly neutrality. It was only some years after her death that he declared that he looked on all creeds with an impartial eye and practised none. With suspension of the Habeas Corpus Act, three of Mullin's Fenian friends were arrested; several others sought safety in exile. Mullin himself took the precaution of leaving home every night (when arrests usually took place) to sleep at the house of an aunt. Fortunately, he was never arrested or detained ... or this story would not have come about.

Aged 22, James took a job in Magherafelt, nine miles from his hometown, pursuing his trade for a more congenial master. The only downside was his two pence a night lodgings, an ill-ventilated, evil-smelling, bug-ridden loft, shared with a tinker, his wife, their two children, and some casual "tramps". As winter approached, his mother suggested that he should stay at home during the cold weather and attend school, to improve his knowledge of the classics. By self-denial, she had saved sufficient money to see them through the winter. Cookstown Academy was one of the finest schools in Ulster, filled with the sons of local gentry, professional men, and prosperous business people. The Principal of the Academy expressed surprise that a cart maker should want to study classics for the sheer love of it and suggested that mathematics would be far more useful in a trade. The tradesman replied that he "much preferred the pleasant to the useful and would probably have never touched the classics if he had considered them to be of the slightest utility." On hearing James' reply, the Principal unhesitatingly agreed to accept him as a pupil for a fee of one guinea a term. For the first time in his life, he had to recognise that there were many people in the world as clever as himself.

Moreover, his handwriting was so bad that he was put to write pothooks, the S-shaped stroke used by children in the initial stage of learning to write. James was undeterred and, at the end of term, the Principal complimented him on his academic performance and refunded half the term's fees. James was also invited to join the senior English class, where his extensive reading served him in good stead, and he stayed at the Academy for another term.

By the time Mullin reached 24, he had a bent back and grey hair, but his determination and application were undiminished. A part-time job at the local government-owned telegraph works gave him employment on Fridays and Saturdays and 10 ten shillings a week. This allowed him to continue his tuition at the Academy for the rest of the week and to support his ageing and ailing mother. The Academy recommended him to try for a literary scholarship at Queen's College, Galway. He obtained a College prospectus and worked earnestly for the examinations, which were 7-8 months away. He was happy to study the set classics books, but he also had to tackle mathematics, a subject he loathed. In 1871, he travelled to Galway to sit the matriculation examination and had the satisfaction of seeing his name placed third on the list of five candidates. He was awarded a scholarship of £30 tenable for one year. He was to stay as a student at Queen's College for nine years.

Things were not easy at Queen's College. Coming from a poor background, Mullin lived frugally to make ends meet and, in the vacations, he returned to Cookstown where he resumed his trade as a carpenter in the telegraph works for thirty shillings a week. Exceptional progress in English, Modern Languages and the Humanities was offset by profound difficulty with mathematics. A failure in that subject in the first end of year exams led to the Council withholding half of his annual scholarship, together with three prizes he had won in English, German and Latin. Undeterred, he successfully resat the mathematics paper in the following autumn and the scholarship money was restored and, after appeal, he regained the prizes. With renewed confidence, he successfully competed for a second scholarship valued at £60. Through hard work, some failures, and a further resit he managed to satisfy his examiners sufficiently to embark on the third year of the degree course, supported by an annual scholarship. At the end of the 1873-4 session he passed his degree in English literature, history and metaphysics with second-class honours, the highest given in those subjects that year. He also won prizes in ancient classics, English literature, history, and metaphysics.

The newly graduated Bachelor of Arts returned home to his devoted mother who was, by that time, becoming infirm and almost blind. She lived long enough to appreciate what they had achieved together before she passed away on 17th October 1874, aged seventy. Her remains were buried at the rear of the old Chapel, Chapel Hill, Cookstown. James Mullin had this to say of his mother: "I am sure I loved her as much as any human being ever loved a mother, and no mother ever lived more worthy of such love. However, beyond that, I revered her as an oracle whose forecasts had never erred, and a mentor whose advice always filled me with hope and courage. During her long life, she never incurred a debt even to the extent of a shilling, and never spent a penny on any superfluities in the way of food and drink. She was a wonderful judge of character, and her prescience, deduced from keen observation, amounted to power that seemed prophetic. Of this she was so conscious that she often said she never liked to predict evil, lest her forecast should prove true."

James sold the family cottage (for £22) and moved to Galway, where he successfully competed for a Senior Scholarship in Modern Languages and Literature, valued at forty pounds. His privations were now at an end - at last, he could enjoy better lodgings, an improved diet, and respectable clothing. He used the money to embark on courses in anatomy, chemistry, botany and zoology, with a view to taking a degree in medicine. He was also able to earn £2-3 a week by teaching classics and, even, mathematics to students preparing for matriculation. He also taught Latin and botany at a young ladies' school and gave private tuition to the son of the Commanding Officer of the Connaught Rangers, an engagement Mullin retained until his career at medical school was almost at an end.

At this point, Mullin allowed himself to be distracted from his goal. Firstly, he embarked on the abortive pursuit for the post of Inspector of Schools, at a salary of £300 a year. He was elected to preside at all the students' sporting meetings and the College Debating Society and he became an occasional anonymous contributor to two Galway newspapers. In addition, Mullin occasionally mixed with Galway's "ne'er-do-wells" and began to show an interest in girls. As he put it himself, he "frittered away in pastime and conviviality a large portion of his time which should have been wholly devoted to preparing for examinations". In addition to this, reckless spending got him into debt. All this had an adverse effect on his medical studies and health. He failed his "half-degree" in medicine on three successive occasions. Two years were wasted, but fortunately, Mullin recognised that he had to pull himself together and get out of the pit into which he was sinking. In the 1877-8 session, he plunged back into his studies, resulting in him winning an Exhibition and a surgery prize. The following year, he won a further Exhibition and a first prize in midwifery. He cut down his coaching engagements to a minimum and, through a friendly physician; he gained the privilege of examining patients on the wards of a local hospital on Sundays. He made friends with the apothecary attached to the County Infirmary, to enhance his knowledge of drugs and therapeutics. At the end of the session, he was awarded a special prize by the Clinical Board, satisfied his examiners and transformed into an M.D. of Queen's College, Queen's University, Ireland, in 1880 ... at the age of 33.

Mullin sought an assistantship in general practice and, through a London agent, he secured a residential vacancy in Brynmawr, at a salary of £60 a year. The large practice had mainly colliery patients, some parish work and a small amount of private work. The senior doctor in the practice quickly recognised his new assistant's clinical ability, excellent bedside manner and popularity with the patients and felt confident enough to take a holiday, leaving James in sole charge. James took the opportunity to learn to ride his master's horse and he eventually became an expert rider.

He subsequently moved to Blaenavon, as an assistant, at a salary of £120 a year, to a former college classmate, Dr. Martin Quirk, who, among other appointments, was chief surgeon to the local works and pits. The 2½ years that Mullin spent in Blaenavon were amongst the hardest of his life, with hard physical and mental toil, little time for rest and incessant night calls. However, they were fruitful years in terms of financial reward, experience, confidence and perhaps surprisingly, pleasure. During this period, he contracted diphtheria from a patient and, on another occasion, he was prohibited from attending general patients in order to give exclusive attention to the victims of a smallpox outbreak. The relationship between Quirk and Mullin developed into a lasting friendship, which continued until the untimely demise of the former. In 1881, Mullin spent a month in Dublin to practise operative surgery under an eminent surgeon and gained the degree of Master of Surgery. On the same visit, he also obtained a Diploma in Midwifery and, in December of that year, Queen's University, conferred upon him the honorary degree of Master in Arts.

Mullin, keen to broaden his experience, took up locum posts in various parts of the country, including an engagement with a Quaker family in Staines, a locum for a Welsh doctor at Ashby de la Zouche, a spell at a sixpenny dispensary in Bristol and more colliery practice in the Ogmore Valley. He now felt ready to set up in practice on his own account. By comparing ratios of doctors to population, he determined that Cardiff was one of the least well-served places and, after a visit, decided to look no further. Shortly after arriving in Cardiff, armed with a letter of introduction, he visited Annie Mary Finco, the English widow of an Italian engineer, in London. On the strength of that meeting, the couple got married on 28th November 1882, spent their honeymoon in Boulogne and set up home in Miskin Street, where their first child, Gladys Mary Celia, was born. By 1886, they

29 Ruthin Gardens

Gordon Hindess

had moved to 29 Ruthin Gardens where their only son, Justin James Patrick, came into the world. Four years later, they made their permanent home at Pendyrys, Conway Road. The corner house at 29 Ruthin Gardens still stands, like most of the terraced houses in this part of Cathays today, part of "studentland". Regrettably, the fine Victorian mansion, Pendyrys, in Conway Road, succumbed to redevelopment about 40 years ago.

After studying the town map, Mullin selected the most central spot on the penny tram system, acquired a small shop at 10 Custom House Street close to it and converted it into a surgery. When he had managed other men's practices, their stinginess with drugs had been a common fault. To address this, he bought in bulk and used cheaper London agents when purchasing drugs from overseas. He had also witnessed countless half-used medicine bottles, so he prescribed in small quantities to minimise waste. Many malicious and unfair complaints were levelled at practitioners for making unnecessary house calls for financial gain, so he made a point of being paid for each house visit at the time, but not calling again unless requested. However, for poor people with a long illness, he would only charge for the first two visits then continue attending without seeking any fee. Although his fees were, lower than that of the average Cardiff doctor, his receipts were probably higher as a result of the volume of work that he did. His daily routine was to see 70-80 patients in his surgery and then make house calls, typically about 20. He slept restlessly, wondering whether he had done the best for his patients and his imagination looked for mistakes. Collecting fees and writing prescriptions became almost automatic and, lacking time for keeping records, he relied on his prodigious memory. His career as a family doctor in Cardiff lasted more than 25 years during which time, with the exception of Sundays and annual holidays; he was never off-duty. On Sundays, he would walk or drive in the countryside, which he found enjoyable and good for his health. His annual holiday was invariably spent walking, with trips to the Lake District, Isle of Man, Scotland and his home country, Ireland. Later, he ventured into Europe, particularly France, where he could eat well at a modest price. A visit to Norway gave him a taste for the sea, which he was never to lose. He particularly enjoyed travelling on small merchant ships, where he could normally dine with the captain and officers, who provided good company and stimulating conversation.

James Mullin

Contemporary Portraits, Western Mail, 1896

Soon after arriving in Cardiff, Mullin resumed his interest in politics, which had been dormant since his student days. He was made vice-chairman of the local branch of the Irish (or National) League , where he encountered a brogue, Catholicism and patriotism stronger than in Ireland, even though most were descendants of the original refugees from the famine. It was through the League that Mullin first came to the notice of the public in Cardiff, when Michael Davitt, a former Fenian, came to deliver a lecture after his release from Portland Prison. The Irish cause was not popular, so there was difficulty in finding a chairman, but Mullin readily accepted the challenge. Although it was the first time that he spoke to a large audience, his carefully prepared speech, conciliatory in tone, was well received. The speech gained him friends in Tory circles and created a lifelong friendship with Davitt, who never came to South Wales without visiting Mullin.

Shortly after, Mullin was appointed Chairman of the local branch of the National League, a position he was to fill for over 25 years. Other distinguished Irishmen would visit him when they came to Cardiff, some as his houseguest. One of these, Charles Stuart Parnell, while staying under his roof, pulled a revolver from his breast pocket, placed it on his bedroom table, and remarked to his host that he had no need to carry the weapon as he was among friends. Dr. Mullin's contribution to Nationalist politics extended beyond Cardiff: he was twice elected to the Executive Councils of the National League in Merthyr and Newport. He was a vice-president of the latter branch and often represented them at the Annual Convention. He had begun life as an uncompromising rebel, but his political views mellowed to the extent that he became a supporter of the British connection and he was strongly critical of the Easter Rebellion, in 1916. In 1895, Dr. Mullin became a Justice of the Peace, in which role he had the reputation for courtesy towards the officers of the court and for dealing with defendants sympathetically and impartially.

While suffering a severe attack of influenza, Mullin realised that he had the symptoms of diabetes. Despite becoming relatively wealthy, his heavy workload was taking a toll on his health and he was finding the work less satisfying. After recovery from the virus, he thought he would continue in practice for another two years, but he changed his mind when a leading consultant offered him the choice of retiring from work immediately or from life entirely. Not surprisingly, Mullin chose the former. Fortunately, a purchaser for the large practice was found, providing him with a modest nest egg. Had it not been sold, his patients would have dispersed among the other Cardiff doctors, with no financial gain to him.

He was not in good health and hoped that a sea voyage would be beneficial. He embarked from Manchester on a Mediterranean cruise. The ship called at Tunis, Malta and Alexandria, from where he visited Cairo and was joined by his wife and sister-in-law. Dr. and Mrs. Mullin toured Cyprus, Beirut, Latakia, and Sidon, where the doctor gave advice and treatment to a patient suffering from typhoid fever. Henceforth, he seldom travelled anywhere without applying his professional expertise. The next port of call was Jaffa, from where they went to Jerusalem. Here, Mullin's scepticism for religion was reinforced by being shown two Mount Calvaries, neither on a hill, and being told about a third in the area. Similarly, he was shown two pools of Bethesda, one of them being a piece of waste-ground where garbage was tipped. He returned to Liverpool, via Algiers, much improved in health and spirits. The following winter he returned to Egypt, spending a whole season there, and, on his way home, called at Athens, a city that fully met his expectations.

Having read that the three most beautiful islands in the world were Jamaica, Java and Ceylon, our doctor put these on his list of places to visit. A trip to the first of these became a reality when the editor of the Western Mail offered to pay the first-class fare in return for a few articles about the island. From lodgings two miles from the centre of the capital, Kingston, he went into the sun-baked city each day, recording features and life. Soon, however, he succumbed to malaria, exhibited in the form of violent fever and nocturnal delirium. He was sensible enough to seek the care of one of the best local doctors and, on his advice, Mullin relocated to a small market town in the hills about 40 miles from Kingston. A few days later an earthquake struck. Mullin and the property, he was staying in were unscathed but, looking in the direction of Kingston, the red glare of a raging fire could be seen. The earthquake had cut off the town but the next day, runners arrived with the news that Kingston was in ruins and

Aftermath of the Kingston Earthquake 1907,
showing burnt-out tram car
Archive postcard

burning. At first light, Mullin travelled by buggy to the nearest station and boarded a goods train bound for Kingston. His objective was to assist with casualties ... and to make a report to his paper. As the train approached its destination, gangs of labourers with shovels, followed by squads of policemen armed with fixed bayonets, crowded into the vans. At every station they passed, the scale of the damage increased: in Kingston, Mullin was unable to identify the streets he had often walked. His own graphic account of the devastation included the following – "a body lying in the sun, burned perfectly black and hard apart from a small patch of white skin on the upper part of the right foot, swarms of flies and the stench of putrefying bodies." The injured lay on the beds or stretched on the grass, much to his surprise, already attended to by doctors and nurses: heads neatly bandaged, fractured limbs in splints. He also noted that the black citizens were far more resolute in adversity than white ones. Although he had ample opportunity to use his camera that day, he declined to do so because it struck him that it would be callous and irreverent. Nevertheless, his eyewitness report was the fullest account of the earthquake and its immediate aftermath to reach the UK. His report also appeared in the Chicago Daily News. Mullin's lodgings in the suburbs of Kingston were demolished, but he managed to retrieve his baggage from the rubble unharmed. After the earthquake, he continued to reside at the hill town, where he was restored to a reasonable state of health.

Despite his experience in Jamaica, Mullin's craving to travel was undiminished. He made several trips to the Canary Islands as ship's surgeon and wrote articles for the press about national exhibitions in various parts of the British Isles including Edinburgh, Glasgow and Dublin. His longest sea voyage as ship's surgeon took him from Glasgow to Durban, Colombo and Rangoon. He ranked Durban as the place he would choose to live if he were compelled to live outside the United Kingdom. He felt most relaxed with the climate, the scenery and the natives of Ceylon, where he found the British residents in Colombo particularly hospitable and friendly. However, Rangoon during the wet season proved depressing and he had to spend most of his time in the hotel, where, as he put it, he managed to "keep body and soul together with doses of quinine and whiskey" – note the Irish spelling! His third and last trip to the Canaries took place in the first year of the First World War, when he was in his late sixties. The conflict then put an end to his travelling.

Throughout his life, Mullin continued to take solace and pleasure from poetry and literature. He was self-effacing about his own poetry, but he wrote a long and prize-winning poem for the National Eisteddfod in 1899, entitled "The Battle of St. Fagans 1648", which he later published. He also wrote the libretto for a composition by a former Mayoress of Cardiff, Mrs. Edward Thomas, called "St. David's Leek" and this appeared in the Western Mail of 28th February 1903. Copies of his patriotic war poem, called "Spirit of Cambria", were sold to raise comforts for the Welsh troops fighting in the First World War. His delight in books is illustrated in "My books" which he wrote for his 56th birthday:

> Companions of my youth and age,
> To you a grateful verse is due,
> For searching over memory's page
> I find no faster friends than you.
> But you, my books exalted high
> Beyond the range of lethal dart!
> Can with a constant light supply
> The darkened chambers of the heart.
> In your companionship I share
> Delight unfailing, of a kind
> That mocks the means of millionaire
> And leaves no bitter taste behind.
> Bless you, my ever-constant friends,
> That change not with the changing wind;
> Your ready sympathy attends
> On every mood that moves the mind.

Mullin considered himself fortunate to have settled in a town with honourable and high-minded colleagues, many of whom became close friends, but he did not join the Cardiff Medical Society. However, as a lover of the open air, he was a member of the Cardiff Naturalists' Society. In his autobiography, he records that old age was the most blissful period of his life. When his wanderlust was curbed by war, he found contentment listening to what he called nature's sweetest music, the prattle of his beloved grandchildren, though the contrast with his own childhood in Cookstown was immense.

Dr. James Mullin, the brilliant and self-made scholar, passed away on 19th December 1919, aged 73 at his home. He had overcome difficulties, which many would find hard to believe, yet had triumphed not only as a doctor, but also as a traveller, author, poet, songwriter, and humourist. His charm and unrivalled gift as a raconteur of his worldwide experiences never failed him, making him a genial companion at all times. He had earned the respect of the citizens of Cardiff, based on good service to his patients, loyalty to the Irish Party in South Wales and an honourable contribution to public life in the city.

Like her husband, Annie became politically involved. As a Liberal Councillor for Roath, she became a member of Women's Liberal Association (WLA), for which she was Cathays Ward Secretary 1891-94 and Cardiff Vice President 1898-1901. Among her guests at "Pendyrys" were Keir Hardie and Viscount Philip Snowden, who was at one time Chancellor of the

Exchequer. Concerned for the welfare of the community, she was an active social worker and, for many years, a member of the Board of Guardians, which administered workhouses. She was a founder member of Cardiff Women's Local Government Association and voted to boycott anti-suffragist liberal candidates, an action which led to the demise of the Cardiff WLA. In 1913, she became chairman of the suffragist Cardiff Progressive Liberal Women's Union. Annie died on 27th January 1921 and was buried with her husband in Cathays Cemetery. Their son, Justin, was educated at a private school in lower Cathedral Road and then Cardiff High School. His determination to follow a military career resulted in him running away to join the Army twice. Eventually, he satisfied this ambition, but died of dysentery in 1908 at the age of 21, while serving with the Royal Lancers in Sialkot, North India. Their elder child, Gladys, a university graduate, married Mr. Iorwerth Clark, an accountant with an estate agency, in Bargoed. Gladys followed in her mother's footsteps and was active in the women's suffrage movement. She died in 1962 and was interred with her parents. There have been two other interments in the family vault - Gladys' daughter, Sybil Clark, in 2015 at the age of 99, and her granddaughter, Nicole Veillard, in 1996, aged 43.

Gordon Hindess

CHAPTER EIGHT

William Harpur (c1853-1917)

William Harpur is buried in Cathays Cemetery along with Mary Ann Harpur, Mary Harpur and Ivor Harpur in Section S, plot 1664. If one enters the Cemetery by the library gate and continues to the third path on the left, one will find his large memorial on the corner, on the left. At the time of writing it is somewhat obscured by vegetation. He was appointed Borough Engineer and Surveyor in 1883, and amongst other things, oversaw the development of isolation facilities on Flat Holm Island.

Flat Holm Cholera Hospital ruins
Cardiff Council Flat Holm Project

Between 1831 and 1866, Cardiff had suffered four outbreaks of cholera and 697 people had died from the disease in the period 1849-1866. In 1883, the decision was made to set up a temporary camp of tents on Flat Holm Island to serve the 900 or so vessels that weekly entered the port. It was never intended to serve the population of Cardiff, for whom a separate Sanatorium would be set up later.

A paddle tug, the Sarah & Jane, was put into service to assist in the work of inspecting vessels bound for Cardiff. Approaching ships would be boarded and inspected and any sufferers would be removed. Initially the use of Flat Holm caused concern: the islanders traded lambs, fowls, eggs, butter, milk and vegetables with the mainland and the value of these would drop if a cholera hospital were positioned alongside the farm. Personnel stationed in the barracks on the island also complained of the risks that they would face. Finally, there were objections from the lighthouse keepers of the risk to navigation if they succumbed to the disease, resulting in the light being extinguished.

Despite these objections, the first cholera victims were received on the island in August 1883 from the steamship, Rishanglys. The port at Newport requested permission to share the facilities, agreeing to pay towards the costs. A further epidemic of cholera broke out in 1892 and five vessels were taken to quarantine moorings off Flat Holm, with patients being removed to the hospital.

By 1895, the facilities were deemed inadequate and the Borough Engineer and Surveyor, William Harpur drew up plans for new hospital buildings. He proposed that provision should only be for cholera patients, with persons of a "superior social position" being isolated from the other patients in smaller wards. Downwater spouts were to be directly connected to rainwater drains, with use of proper hospital pattern slop sinks. He also proposed using solid window frames, which were less liable to harbour dust and germs. Extractor ventilators were to have vertical shafts through the roof.

Agreement was reached for the facilities to be shared with Barry, and later by Barnstaple, Bridgwater and Watchet, although by 1931 Barnstaple and Watchet were only contributing £1 per annum. The use of the hospital was extended to victims of yellow fever and plague. In 1900, one person was actually recorded to have died from bubonic plague and was cremated in the hospital's crematorium. In 1936/37, the hospital was closed and Caerau Isolation Hospital, built in 1928, took over its responsibilities.

In Cardiff itself, working in co-operation with William Wallace Pettigrew, Head Gardener to Cardiff Corporation and later to become Parks Superintendent, William Harpur was responsible for designing and laying out the infrastructure for Roath, Grange and Victoria Parks. At Roath Park, where the Marquis of Bute and others had donated land in 1887, the creation of the lake from an area of marshland was a significant engineering feat. There was a grand opening ceremony in 1894. For Grange Park, the low-lying land had to be raised using refuse and scalpings before the park was laid out and planted, eventually opening to the public in 1895. Victoria Park was laid out on the site of the former Ely Common, opening in 1897.

Grange Park

Gordon Hindess

The other park, which owes much to Harpur, is Cathays Park. After protracted negotiations, Cardiff Corporation acquired the land from the Marquis of Bute for a prestigious civic centre in 1897. Again working with W W Pettigrew, Harpur drew up plans for the park in 1897 and the area was developed progressively thereafter.

From around 1883, Solomon Andrews, one of Cardiff's leading Victorian entrepreneurs, had been pursuing schemes to redevelop Edward Haycock's market, which dated from 1835, and much of the adjacent frontage of St Mary Street. In 1884 he took a lease on a substantial street frontage, including the market entrance, and proceeded with the erection of a huge new building with four floors which at the time, dwarfed adjoining buildings. This building included the St Mary's Street market entrance, which we see today.

In 1890, Haycock's market closed for demolition and, in August of that year, a memorial stone was laid for the new market, which was officially opened on 8 May 1891, by the Lady Mayoress, the Marchioness of Bute. A plaque to commemorate the occasion can still be seen near the Trinity Street entrance – but it is not easily visible.

Commemorative Plaque in Cardiff Market

Gordon Hindess

The new Central Market was designed by William Harpur, consisting of a large wrought iron shed running from the back wall of Market Buildings through to Trinity Street. In all,

Trinity Street Market Entrance

Gordon Hindess

349 stalls were provided in the original layout, and there was a raised office for the market superintendent on the ground floor surmounted by a clock tower.

As a chartered engineer, Harpur was active in local professional institutions, presenting papers, etc. He was involved in significant drainage schemes around the city, which were contributing to the improvement of public health. An excellent example of his work can be found in the Pumping Station, Penarth Road, next to the River Ely.

This red and yellow brick building originally housed pumps, driven by huge beam engines, to help sewage from the western side of Cardiff on its way to eventual discharge to the Severn Estuary off Lavernock Point. If one heads out from the city centre for this building, look out for Harpur Street on the right of Penarth Road, just after the entrance to Brains Brewery.

The Pumping Station, Penarth Road

Gordon Hindess

Harpur also takes credit for planning the tramway network and the construction of Lansdowne Hospital, in 1895, as the treatment and isolation unit for infectious diseases.

Harpur Street nameplate

Gordon Hindess

One is entitled to ask whether an overgrown grave in Cathays Cemetery and having his name on one of the least significant streets in the city represent adequate recognition for someone who contributed so much of enduring value to Cardiff.

Paul Jones and Gordon Hindess

CHAPTER NINE

The Cardiff Pals

It was not generally the practice to repatriate casualties during World War I so we are particularly honoured to have two of the "Cardiff Pals" buried at Cathays Cemetery. They are Bernard Bastable, Pte 14576, who died 14th May 1916, born in Radstock, Somerset, and buried in plot EH 2162, from the Welsh Regiment, Depot and Windsor Phillips, Pte 14139, 2nd July 1915, born in Cardiff, and buried in plot EF 8572 in Cathays Cemetery, from the 11th Battalion, Welsh Regiment. This is their story.

At its outset, the First World War was expected to be a great adventure leading to a swift and inevitable British victory. As a result, many young men wanted to volunteer and to gain a share in the glory. However, many such men wanted to serve alongside their pals, their friends from work or from the same town.

The Cardiff Pals were put together in the five weeks following the outbreak of war. Over 800 men under the age of 30 had put themselves forward. Many were never to return. A recruit had to be over 5 feet 3 inches in height, at least 34 inches around the chest and between 19 and 30 years old. Many men from the same firm joined the Pals together and many employers such as the local firm of Howells made it known that they would reinstate those who joined once the war was over.

It was a sunny Monday morning on September 14th 1914, when the Cardiff Pals Commercial Battalion, the 11th Welsh, marched in fours, from Maindy Barracks to Cardiff General Station. Most men carried a suitcase or parcel. Throngs of children and weeping women cheered them on. Their destination was Lewes, a market town on the South Downs where their training would begin. Due to the large numbers of enlistees, uniforms and drill guns were in short supply and many had to go without whilst training at Lewes. When the uniforms did eventually arrive, the Pals were nicknamed by the other units as "the Chocolate Soldiers" on account of their smart appearance.

The billets were now switched to Hastings and it was here that Private Windsor Phillips aged 19 died during training. In April 1915, the men were moved to Aldershot in order to shape them as a fighting unit, by carrying out more serious training. Both Kitchener and King George V inspected the 11th Welsh whilst at Aldershot.

On September 4th 1915, the Pals sailed from Southampton to Le Havre in two ships, the Princess Victoria and the Bellaraphon. It was Wales going to war. In September 1915, they saw their first action and on September 21st their first casualty of the war, Lance-corporal Alfred Johnson, aged 24, hit by a shell.

In October 1915, the Bulgarians sided with the Central Powers against the Allies and

Memorial to Windsor Phillips

Paul Jones

that same month the Pals were embarked on the Megantic for an 11-day voyage to Salonika, a sun-drenched city with waterfront buildings and minarets. The Somme with its rat-infested trenches now seemed far away. Now the men were to suffer the dust and heat of the Macedonian hills whilst at night the temperatures would fall below freezing. Their task was to fortify Salonika into a defence known as the "Birdcage": road making, trench digging and the odd route march to break the monotony was the order of the day. However, the Pals actually saw little of the city of Salonika, most being lucky if they spent one weekend there in three years. Reality was in hard work and boredom.

Meanwhile Cardiff families had organised to send "comforts" of cigarettes, tobacco, Oxo cubes and warm clothing like socks and mittens to the boys at the front. Men from a division sent earlier to Salonika had been sent to the front line with only tropical kit. Many were brought down by mule transport to base hospitals suffering from frostbite. Many died.

The June 1916 issue of the Cardiff Pals Magazine recorded the following: "The committee representing the Relatives and Friends as well as the boys at Salonika placed a beautiful wreath of laurels and flowers upon the coffin of Private Bernard Bastable with the words "Duty Done, Victory Won" together with the Regimental Badge embossed in silver".

Originally, an employee of Howells Department Store, Bernard Bastable had enlisted in September 1914. In Salonika, he caught a chill and was sent to St Davids Hospital, Malta. He was transferred to Edward VII Hospital Cardiff (near the Royal Infirmary) for treatment to his ears but after suffering terrible pain, he died suddenly on May 14th 1916. His elder brother Percy Bastable remained with the Pals in Salonika.

The Pals moved up to Jenikol in the mountains on August 3rd 1916 for trench duty patrol work against the Bulgarians. Work

Memorial to Bernard Bastable

Paul Jones

commenced on a tunnel linking the front to the rear trenches at Wave Hill. Malaria then took its toll on the battalions, knocking the 11th Welsh down to about 600 men. Some battalions suffered so badly that they were even withdrawn from the line.

October 22nd 1916 saw a Victoria Cross awarded to Private H W Stokey Lewis for valour in a raid on enemy trenches on the Piton des Mitrailleuses (Machine Gun Hill) and the Dorsale, a ridge running off it.

At the end of 1916, the Pals, now in Bulgaria, confronted a Bulgarian army under its German officers and NCOs at Pip Ridge and the Grand Couranne. The latter was a type of medieval castle overlooking Lake Dorian. The fighting here was to last three grim years and, in April and May 1917, over 6,000 British troops were killed or wounded during assaults. On September 18th 1918, the 11th Battalion of the Welsh Regiment, amongst others, spearheaded an attack on the hilltop fortress. At 5.08am, as the British artillery barrage lifted, Captain Eynon punted his rugby ball at the enemy, and the Cardiff Pals went up the hill ... By 8am, the 11th Welsh ceased to exist. However, eventually, the Bulgarians fled their entrenchments and the Hill was taken.

The surviving Pals formed the Pals Old Boys Association, holding an Annual Dinner at the Park Hotel into the 1960s.

We are indebted to John Evan Davies and Ken Cooper for the stories contained in their publication "Cardiff Pals".

Paul Jones

CHAPTER TEN

Unravelling the Cory Web

There are Corys buried in at least four locations in Cathays Cemetery. Two Cory families came from the West Country, in the eighteenth century, and went on to build substantial businesses, which had many similarities. Both started in shipping, both became prominent Cardiff citizens and benefactors and some family members shared the same first names. It is not surprising that some historians have confused the two families. Our objective here is to dispel any misunderstandings.

The Bideford Family

The Cardiff story starts with the arrival of Richard Cory, from Bideford, around 1838. He was the owner of a small vessel trading between Cardiff, Bristol and Ireland, but he opened a ship chandlery in Cardiff, near the Custom House. At the same time, he brought over his wife and

Richard and Sarah Cory's Memorial

Gordon Hindess

three young sons, John aged 10, Richard aged 8 and Thomas aged 5. While still in their teens, the two elder sons joined the business, which then traded as Richard Cory and Sons, describing themselves as shipbrokers, ship owners, coal merchants and exporters. Richard Cory (the elder) retired in 1859, at the age of 60, relatively young for those times. His wife, Sarah Marks Cory, died on October 6th 1868, aged 66, but Richard had a long retirement, dying on May 5th 1882, aged 82. Although Cathays Cemetery had opened a few years before Sarah's death, she and her husband were buried in Adamsdown Cemetery, Cardiff's first municipal cemetery. This site was converted to a cemetery park around 1970 and the headstones were moved into small arcs in the corners and in the centre, to create a large open space. By 2006, the park was looking decidedly run-down, so was given a facelift. The makeover included a new entrance from Moira Terrace, a memorial path, new trees and seats and a games and activity area designed by and for local youngsters. The headstone from the Cory grave survived these changes and can be found by the memorial path near the centre of the park.

After the father's retirement, the business was re-named Cory Brothers & Co and it became a limited liability company in 1888. The following year, its new home, Corys' Buildings, opened on the corner of Bute Street and Bute Place. Among the many prestigious buildings in the commercial heart of 19th Century Cardiff, this was one of the grandest and remains today as a grade II listed building, which is being incorporated into the Merchant Place re-development as Cory Chambers.

The sons, John and Richard became coal owners in their own right with the purchase of Pentre colliery in the Rhondda, in 1868. Other collieries in the Rhondda, Cynon, Neath and

Corys' Buildings
Gordon Hindess

Ogmore valleys were later acquired, and the brothers also became the largest private wagon owners in the UK. With the universal demand for Welsh steam coal for shipping, and especially after the opening of the Suez Canal in 1869, the firm established coaling stations, offices and agencies around the world. By 1908, they had 118 depots on all the major shipping routes. John was also a founder and vice-chairman of the Barry Dock and Railway. They supplied coal

Cory Memorial Temperance Hall
Courtesy of Cardiff Central Library Local Studies Section

on a worldwide basis, most of it coming from their collieries in the Rhondda. In 1942, the company was bought by the Powell Duffryn Group, but maintained its identity as a shipping agent, offering a comprehensive range of services for shipowners, charterers and traders around the world. The local office is in St Mellons today.

By seizing the opportunities offered by the demand for steam coal and improved methods of transport, the family prospered immensely. However, they were also great benefactors, assisting all kinds of movements, which helped social, educational and moral reform. Richard Cory (the

elder) became a leader of the United Methodist church in Cardiff, John was a Wesleyan and Richard (the younger) a Baptist, but all gave assistance to the Salvation Army and the temperance movement. Their support for the latter was manifest in the Cory Memorial Temperance Hall (pictured on the previous page), in Station Terrace (near Queen Street Station), which was built as a memorial to his father by John. Opened in September 1896, it was given over to the Cardiff Temperance Hall Trust to administer. Sadly, it was demolished in the early 1980s to make way for the Capitol shopping centre.

For many years before his death, John Cory's benefactions amounted to nearly £50,000 a year and, in memory of his work for the people of Cardiff, his bronze statue, designed by Sir William Goscombe John, was erected in the city in 1905. It is in the Gorsedd Gardens and shows him with a Bible in his hand.

John Cory statue in the Gorsedd Gardens, Cardiff

Gordon Hindess

It was John Cory (1828-1910) who had the present house at Dyffryn, St. Nicholas, built. There had been houses on the site since the Middle Ages and John acquired the estate from the Bruce-Pryce family in 1893 and promptly set about rebuilding the house. On his death, the house passed to his third son, Reginald, a distinguished amateur horticulturist, who was largely responsible, with the landscape architect Thomas Mawson, for creating the important gardens that surround Dyffryn House today. The estate was leased to Glamorgan County Council in June 1939 and stewardship passed to the Vale of Glamorgan Borough Council as a result of local government reorganisation. A 50-year lease to the National Trust, which took effect in January 2013, promises improved management of the gardens and much needed restoration of the house.

In 1907, John would have seen another of his children, Sir Clifford, created 1st Baronet of Llantarnum Abbey, where he had made his home. Although Clifford

Dyffryn House

Gordon Hindess

obtained a commission in the Welsh Regiment, his principal career was in the family coal business, of which he was to become chairman. He was also a proud Liberal, being a member of Glamorgan County Council for nearly 20 years and notable as the only substantial coal owner to maintain a prominent political profile in the Rhondda at this time. He stood for parliament a number of times, initially without success, but eventually gained the seat of St Ives, in Cornwall. At various times, he was chairman of the Monmouthshire and South Wales Coal Owners Association, the South Wales and Monmouthshire Schools of Mines and the Welsh Coal Trade Conciliation Board. He was also President of Cardiff Incorporated Chamber of Commerce, President of Cardiff Liberals, High Sheriff of Monmouthshire, a Justice of the Peace for Glamorgan and Monmouthshire and a Deputy Lieutenant of the County of Glamorgan. In his personal life, Clifford was a keen sportsman and a particularly good polo player - his name appears frequently in the sporting news section of The Times, he played for an England team against the French and he appeared for the House of Commons team and the Hurlingham Club. He died childless in 1941, at the age of 81, so the baronetcy died with him. The house was requisitioned during World War II but then, more appropriately to its name, became the property of the Sisters of St. Joseph of Annecy, in 1946. However, Clifford is perhaps best remembered for the financial assistance that he gave to the "Ton Pentre Temperance" brass band, which changed its name to "The Cory Band" in consequence.

Walk into section L on the higher path from the chapels and one cannot miss a prominent red granite obelisk on the right marking the vault of Richard (the younger) Cory and his family. As well as Richard, who died in 1914 aged 84, the vault also holds his wife, Emily, who was 87 when she died in 1919. In addition, the memorial records five children who died in infancy and a sole son, Richard Vivian, who reached adulthood but was interred in Bloemfontein, where he died from wounds received in action in 1900.

Richard Cory memorial obelisk
Gordon Hindess

The Padstow Family

John Cory, born in 1823, was the head of the family that moved to Cardiff from Padstow. Although this John Cory was the son of a farmer, he went to sea and, in 1854, established his own business by purchasing a coastal ketch. He steadily built up his fleet of sailing ships and, in 1863, retired from the sea in order to manage this fleet from an office in Padstow. One of his early and lucrative contracts was the transport of Cornish granite to build the Thames Embankment. In the 1860s, with the silting of the estuary of the Camel and declining cargoes, Padstow was becoming a maritime backwater and, in 1872, John Cory and his family

John Cory & Sons Building,
James Street, built in 1898

Gordon Hindess

moved to the rapidly growing port of Cardiff. It is worth noting here that, with the son of Richard from Bideford, there were now two John Corys in town of similar age.

The John Cory from Padstow was one of the earliest owners of steamships in Cardiff and the rise of his company was rapid. His sons, John (yet another one, henceforth refer to as John II) and James Herbert, joined the business, which was then known as John Cory & Sons. By 1876, the fleet had grown to 10 vessels; in 1898, this had increased to 23 with the business interests including ship brokering, iron ore merchants, timber importers and coal exporters. In that year, too, the company built the offices one can see today on the corner of Mount Stuart Square and James Street

John, the elder, died on 11th December 1891 and joined his sole daughter, Beatrice Maud, who had died at the age of seven weeks in 1873. John's place of death is recorded as St. Julians, Newport, although his home for much of his later life had been in Penarth. His wife, Jemima, died in 1905 and is the only other occupant of the family vault. If one heads down the centre path southwestwards through Section M, the memorial on the vault is towards the end and a little way off to the left. The red granite obelisk, topped by a grey granite column should be easy to spot with its distinctive symbolism, an anchor of hope (so popular with seafarers) and a broken column, signifying life cut short, possibly reflecting the death of Beatrice, the first interment here.

However, where are the two sons? If one continues in a southwesterly direction to the smaller, triangular part of Section W, John Cory II's burial place is at the first corner of that triangle reached. However, the memorial does not stand out. Indeed, the author of one book assumed that it signified a wish to be less ostentatious than his father did. The real reason is that it falls in an area where lawn conversion was carried out in the 1960s. This process was carried out nationwide until, fortunately, legal action elsewhere brought it to a halt. The objective was to make cemetery maintenance easier and cheaper. This was achieved by taking headstones from alternate rows and putting them at the foot of the plot, creating double rows

John Cory, the elder, memorial

Gordon Hindess

of back-to-back memorials. Kerbs were removed completely and large memorials (of which John II's was one) were replaced by smaller rudimentary concrete ones, typically recording only a surname and burial year or years. The original inscriptions were recorded and the information is deposited in the National Archive, in Kew.

John Cory II

Gordon Hindess

The monument consists of a small cream headstone with the inscription CORY with three dates, 1899, and 1931 twice. The first date marks the death of their daughter Mary Rosalie, who died at the age of 21. John and his wife Emma died in the same year, 1931. We know from the National Archive records that the original memorial included "White marble cross, four bases and kerbs" and that the family home was at Seaview House, Bradford Place, Penarth. While this property no longer exists, being high above Penarth Head, it would have lived up to its name. In 1933, the family donated the house to the National Children's Home, where it served to accommodate 36 girls aged 12 to 16. In March 1941, the home was severely damaged in an air raid and closed for the rest of the war. However, the building was repaired and the home re-opened after the war, continuing in operation until 1960. Today the site is occupied by flats.

John II was 17 when he came to Cardiff. He married Emma, the daughter of George Hosking Wills, who coincidentally came from Bideford (where the other Cory family hailed from!), and they had seven children. John was a director of some thirty-six shipping, ship-repairing and trading companies, a staunch Conservative, but not an active politician, and a Wesleyan Methodist. He was 86 when he died, his wife about two years younger. They left two sons, John Herbert, who died in 1939, aged 50, and Charles Kingsley, who died in 1967, aged 77. They also had four other daughters all of whom married, two of them into another big Cardiff ship owning family, the Morels.

We have seen that Corys were quick to recognise that the future was in steam-powered ships. They were also innovative (and shrewd) in the way they built up their fleet. Vessels were acquired by setting up single-ship companies. The cost of each ship was divided up into a large number of shares, which were promoted by means of a prospectus and newspaper adverts. However, shares in ships were high-risk. Investors could be ruined if a vessel did not run at a profit. However, the manager (i.e. the Cory's business) was paid a percentage of gross earnings: as long as the ship was working - even if not making a profit – it would make money. At the outbreak of the First World War, John Cory & Sons had 23 ships and a worldwide market for its unique blend of coal, "Cory's Pacific Navigation Large Steam Coal". During the war, 20 Cory vessels were sunk and at the end of the war, they emerged with nine ships. Between the wars, merchant ships became bigger and the Cory fleet smaller. In the

Second World War, they lost the three ships with which they started the war and one bought as a replacement was sunk on her second trip. After the war, they chartered a steamship for two years and then, between 1948 and 1954, bought two more ships. The company ceased ship owning in 1966.

We must not overlook John II's younger brother, (James) Herbert! If we turn right at the junction, where we found John II, then Herbert's memorial is close by the next corner. Again, it is a replacement concrete marker, but it may prove more difficult to spot, because there is more vegetation in the vicinity and lichen on the headstone makes the name "Cory" at the top hard to see. The remaining inscription is clearer, the three lines reading Elizabeth 1908, James Herbert 1933 and Elizabeth Cansh 1957. Since they were all Corys, it is not clear why dates were not considered sufficient, as with John II's replacement stone. Could it be that someone thought that Herbert and Cansh were separate family names? Again, we know from the National Archive records that the original memorial included "grey granite kerbs and white marble figure."

Herbert's first wife, Elizabeth, was the sister of John II's wife and they had four sons and one daughter. Elizabeth died in 1908 and, two years later, Herbert married Elizabeth Cansh Walker, an appreciably younger woman, with whom he had two more daughters. Herbert, like his brother, was a director of many companies involved in shipping and trading and a committed Christian but, unlike his brother, he took an active interest in politics: he became Conservative MP for Cardiff in 1915 and for Cardiff South 1918-23 and served as sheriff of Glamorgan in 1913. With his brother, he founded a scholarship at the Cardiff Technical College and he devoted his salary as MP to the funds of the King Edward VII Hospital and the Hamadryad Seamen's Hospital. In 1900, he had the impressive Coryton House built: it is from this that the current northern part of Whitchurch takes its name. Initially, a small garden was laid out around the house with an orchard, walled garden, glasshouse and pond. However, by 1940, under the hand of his second wife, a much more expansive layout was created, with terraced gardens adjoining the house and, below these, an informal area including cascades, pools and exotic plantings of conifers and bamboos. Sadly, the gardens have largely given way to new development - houses, a hotel and a superstore, but the house is still there, having been reincarnated as a civil defence headquarters for Cardiff, a Post Office (and, later, BT) training centre and now a residential school for young people with autism.

Herbert Cory memorial

Gordon Hindess

Herbert's contribution to public life was recognised by elevation to the peerage in 1919, as 1st Baronet Coryton. In which role, he took an active part, fully supported by his second wife. We find that, as Lady Elizabeth Cansh Cory, she was presented at Court by Dame Margaret Lloyd George, in 1922. One can find the formal photographs, which commemorated the occasion in the Victoria and Albert Museum. The baronetcy passed to his eldest son, Herbert George Donald, then to his eldest son, Vyvyan Donald Cory. When Vyvyan was killed in action in 1941, his younger brother, Clinton James Donald became 4th baronet and his son, Sir Clinton Charles Donald Cory, the 5th baronet, carried the title into the 21st century. In his late seventies, he lives in Hertfordshire.

Ty Coryton

Orbis Education & Care

As this illustrates, the male succession is stronger in the Padstow family than the Bideford one. There are grandchildren and great grandchildren to be found around Glamorgan today ... and further afield, including the USA. While it is beyond the scope of this book to continue a detailed family history, it is worth recording a few glimpses into it.

We find another John Cory in the fourth generation. He was educated at Eton and Cambridge, became one of the youngest High Sheriffs in Britain (for Glamorgan), and was appointed a Deputy Lieutenant, then Vice Lieutenant of South Glamorgan in 1990. In the Church in Wales, he was a member of the Governing Body from 1957 to 1974, and of the Representative Body from 1960. He was appointed a Knight of St John in 1968. He was chairman of Cardiff Rural District Council from 1971 to 1972, and chairman of the Tax Commissioners for Cardiff District. Unusually, he had a problem with physical co-ordination, which, amongst other things, meant that "he was exceptionally unsafe in any boat and regularly fell into ponds, lakes and rivers." However, he was perhaps best known in the worlds of hunting, horse breeding and racing. He served as president of the National Light Horse Breeding Society and a vice-chairman of the Sport Horse Breeding Society of Great Britain. He was married to Sarah Meade, the sister of the Olympic eventing rider Richard Meade.

Just a few years ago, two members of the fifth generation had a minor reunion at Coryton House. John (that name again!) Cory, a retired financial director and secretary of the Wales Tourist Board from Pentyrch met with James Cory, a retired stockbroker from Hungerford, the event being initiated following contact by a relative in the USA who was tracing the family history.

Charles Raymond, a fourth-generation Cory, was educated at Harrow and read Law at Oxford. In the Second World War, he saw action as an able seaman on Arctic convoy duties and, having been commissioned as a sub-lieutenant RNVR, on North Atlantic convoys. He was on the frigate Retalick, which served as an escort during the Normandy landings in

June 1944, and received the commander-in-chief's commendation for his role in the rescue of American troops from a stricken landing craft. The burning vessel's ammunition was exploding; sending shells in all directions, but Cory and two seamen went over Retalick's side and swam out with lifelines to bring survivors to safety. After demobilisation, Raymond became a director of John Cory & Sons and then served as chairman for 26 years, as the business became that of shipbroker and agent and diversified into travel agency, garages and a stake in Cambrian Airways. He was chairman of Milford Haven Port Authority and the Pilotage Authorities of Barry and Port Talbot; on a national level, he was a member of the council of Lloyd's Register and vice-chairman of the British Transport Docks Board. Outside of these maritime roles, he was also vice-chairman of AB Electronics, the first chairman of South Glamorgan Health Authority and, later, chairman of the council of the University of Wales College of Medicine. In 1954, he published "A Century of Family Shipowning", the story of the family business.

It has been suggested that these two Cory families are distantly related, but it would require further research into their lives in the West Country before the nineteenth century to confirm this. What is beyond dispute is that, together, they made a tremendous contribution to the development and prosperity of Cardiff and have left a legacy that can still be appreciated today.

Simplified Cory Family trees are provided in the Appendix.

Gordon Hindess

CHAPTER ELEVEN

A Remarkable Engineer

Charles Lafayette Hunter MICE, MIME, MIMA was born in Tredegar on 29th October 1839 and he died on 8th February 1902, in Penarth. His story must begin with an exploration of his middle name.

Charles Lafayette Hunter
Contemporary Portraits, Western Mail, 1896

In the early years of the nineteenth century, a Samuel Thomas Hunter and his wife, Ann Fiott, moved to Tredegar, South Wales. They had married in 1798 and had six children. The last of these children born in 1812 was Charles Hunter, who married Mary Rees in 1832 and was the father of our illustrious engineer. As was common at the time, they named their son Charles Fiott Hunter to show the ancestral family origins. It is thought that his grandmother Ann Fiott (or Fiatt) was part of the Marquis de Lafayette family, who on moving to Jersey, Channel Islands, anglicised their name, it being the period of the Napoleonic Wars.

By the time he was married on the 2nd December 1862, Charles had changed his middle name to Lafayette, which would suggest that the family legend linking back to the Marquis would have been confirmed at that time.

The young Charles was educated in Long Ashton, Bristol, following which he was apprenticed at the Tredegar Ironworks Company in 1853, where his father held a position and his uncle Thomas Ellis was coming to the end of 25 years as Chief Engineer. In 1829, the founder of the ironworks, Samuel Homfray, had sent Thomas Ellis with another to view the inventions of George Stephenson, now famous for his development of steam locomotives, about which very little was known at the time. As a result of Ellis's visit, the best steam locomotives were introduced to the South Wales area. Initially three were purchased and later others were assembled at the ironworks and eventually by 1853, eleven had been built there.

As early as 1829, Thomas Ellis drove the first locomotive the 28 miles along the plated tramway to Newport. In preparation, two men were sent in advance to cut down any overhanging tree branches but the wayward couple abandoned their work at Tredegar Park in Newport and retired to a local hostelry. Unknown to Ellis, the Stephenson Flyer proceeded assuming all work was complete and on travelling through the park area, the tall chimney of the engine was broken off by a low limb of a trackside tree.

At that time, most boys would have received just a rudimentary schooling in the locality of their home so the young Charles entered his apprenticeship at an enormous advantage having been a boarder at Long Ashton for a number of years. Indeed so much so that he attained the position of Chief Engineer of Tredegar Ironworks and Locomotive Superintendent of the Sirhowy Railway Company, the position previously held by his uncle, in the year of his twenty first birthday.

Modernisation of the 28 mile plated tramroad became essential in the early days of his appointment. The plate ways were replaced with rails and all the locomotives and rolling stock were fitted with flanged wheels in place of plain ones.

In 1856, Henry Bessemer had invented his converter to change iron to steel and demand for iron products declined. As well as the high costs involved the local iron ore contained too much phosphorous for successful steel making. Eventually the ironworks closed at the end of the nineteenth century.

Charles resigned his post in 1874. The Sirhowy Railway Company, struggling to recover from the costs of converting their tramroad, was selling out to a major railway company and coal mining was booming.

Between 1850 and 1900, South Wales coal production increased from 10 million to 40 million tons per year. Sourced from the thick seams of steam coal in the Taff, Rhondda and Cynon valleys, port facilities enabling export were developed at Cardiff.

The Bute West Dock was completed in 1839 followed by the East in 1859 and Roath Basin in 1874. In 1876, Charles Lafayette Hunter was appointed to the post of Chief Mechanical Engineer to the Bute Docks.

There was great competition for the coal trade between coalmines, railways and ports. Some enterprises had interests in a combination of all three. Until 1865, port handling of coal coming down the Taff valley had been a monopoly. The opening of Penarth Dock by the Taff Vale Railway Company changed that situation. There were also proposals in the 1860s, which did not come to fruition, to develop Barry with a direct rail link to the coalfields.

By 1880 with 8 million tons of coal passing through the Bute Docks there was immense congestion, which resulted in Parliamentary approval to construct a further dock, Roath Dock. To finance this an additional one penny per ton would be charged at all the Cardiff docks. Tired of delays and spiralling costs, coal and ship owners successfully obtained the right to construct a dock at Barry and the Barry Railway through to the Rhondda, which were completed in their entirety by 1889.

The need to increase efficiency, safety and quality of coal in the holds of ships brought

The new system of moveable cranes designed by Charles Lafayette Hunter

Associated British Ports

about a revolutionary method of loading. Hitherto coal was tipped some four feet into a chute rolling twenty-four feet until it fell up to thirty feet into the ship's hold. As well as excessive breakage, accumulations of gases were retained under the tipped coal leading to combustion later. Trimmers worked in the holds to distribute the load and for a time the ship could be dipped from the head or the stern. Mid loading, the ship had to move for hatch alignment.

The new system consisted of moveable cranes that lined up with each of the ship's hatches and placed the coal around the hold and the specially designed crane hopper released the coal no more than two feet from the floor or cargo. On the quayside, the full ten-ton load of each railway wagon was tilted to tip the coal a few feet into the carrying box. The cranes were also used to unload incoming cargo. The new Roath Dock was fitted with this facility and was declared by shippers to be the best in the world. The system was patented in 1887 in the names of Sir William Thomas Lewis, the docks manager, and Charles Lafayette Hunter, of 205 Newport Road, Cardiff, Engineer. A model is on show at the Maritime Museum in Swansea.

Whilst Charles' name was most prominent in engineering circles for the new loading system, the building of locomotives, extensive alterations and additions to mechanical appliances were carried out under his direction.

In 1897, Charles was appointed Chief Engineer to the Cardiff Railway Company, the new name for the Bute Docks Company, created to mirror the Barry arrangement of having a direct line to the coalfields. However, it was only in 1909, after his death, that this became operational.

Another project not seen through to fruition was the construction of the new dock. Coal exports were still expanding and the need for more facilities and to accommodate larger ships capable of loads

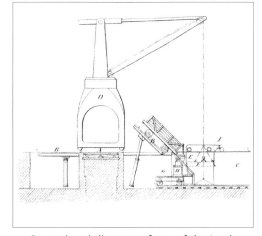

Operational diagram of one of the Lewis-Hunter moveable cranes

Malby & Sons, Photo-Litho 1886

in excess of 6,000 tons were apparent. The patented loading system lent itself to this task loading 400 tons per hour with two cranes in use.

Together with Mr. G. M. Abernethy, Consulting Engineer of London, Charles was responsible for the design of what eventually in 1907 was named as The Queen Alexandra Dock.

Charles Lafayette Hunter was a Member of the Institutions of Civil Engineering, of Mechanical Engineering and of Naval Architecture. He was invited on many occasions to put his name forward for Municipal duties but always refused. As Chief Engineer, his priority was to his duty and to the management of the 300 to 400 staff employed. He respected them and they benefited from his sense of justice and fairness.

His funeral took place on 11th February 1902. Watched by many, the six coaches progressed through the streets from his home in Penarth to Cathays Cemetery where he was interred in plot L1159 just along from the Episcopal Chapel. In memory of him, Hunter Street in an area of Cardiff Bay then known as Rat Island was given his name.

Thanks are extended to Mr. Tom Mutter of Rhiwbina Cardiff and other family members from whom the information for this story was obtained.

Ivor Lippett

CHAPTER TWELVE

Scandal at the Bank

At the beginning of the nineteenth century, numerous savings banks were being established, often with philanthropic principles, to encourage thrifty habits amongst the growing working and artisan classes. One such bank was the Cardiff Savings Bank.

The "Cardiff Government Security Savings' Bank" to give it its full name, was founded in 1818 twelve months after the passing of Rose's Act which allowed small savings banks to invest their surplus funds in government bonds or deposit them at the Bank of England. The Act also specified the duties of trustees and managers, none of whom could derive personal benefit from the bank, and was intended to create trust amongst potential depositors. The bank started trading in Wharton Street and grew steadily, matching Cardiff's growing population. Its growth was aided by the lack of competition from other institutions that catered for the "thrifty poor" who welcomed a safe place for their small deposits.

In 1846, it was decided to seek larger and more convenient premises and so a site at the junction of Duke St and North Rd, next to the castle was purchased from the 2nd Marquess of Bute for £400. Five years later James Emerson Williams was appointed Actuary to the bank, a post he would hold for 35 years until his death.

Born in Cardiff in 1815, James Emerson Williams was the son of an army sergeant major, a gifted mathematician, who seems to have passed on this skill on to his son. His career started as a schoolmaster in Cardiganshire, where he met and married Caroline Ferrier, the daughter of a noted local family, but soon moved to Swansea to assist his father who was by now actuary of the Swansea Savings Bank. Eventually they left Swansea and he became a reporter with the Cardiff and Merthyr Guardian, ultimately becoming its editor, a position he held for some years until his appointment as Actuary of the Cardiff Savings Bank.

He died aged 70 on 26th March 1886 after an illness of only three months, and was buried in Cathays Cemetery four days later. The obituary published in the Western Mail was extensive and praised both his personal and professional qualities:

"Mr Williams was widely known in Cardiff and was universally respected. He was a gentleman of very kindly disposition, and being brought, as he was day by day, into contact with large numbers of people who had business at the savings' bank, he became known to an unusually wide circle. His unfailing courtesy and kindliness of manner endeared him to all, whilst his business qualities and the knowledge he possessed of banking affairs made him invaluable as an Actuary ... Under his able supervision the bank attained a high degree of prosperity and his services would be greatly missed by the gentlemen who assisted him in the management of the concern, and whose confidence he most fully enjoyed."

However, on 24th April 1886, less than a month after the death of Mr Williams, there was much consternation in the streets of Cardiff when the following notice was placed on the door of the bank in Duke Street.

CARDIFF SAVINGS BANK

Notice

The trustees and managers having discovered several acts of dishonesty in the accounts of the late actuary, Mr James Emerson Williams, deem it prudent to suspend business until the accounts of the bank have been thoroughly investigated. In the meantime the trustees and managers are happy to be able to inform the public that the principal part of the funds of the bank, about £160,000, are safely secured in the hands of the Comptroller-General

For the Trustees and Managers

April 24th 1886   J Marshall

Investors congregated outside the bank exchanging stories of their losses and lucky escapes, and wondering how such a state of affairs had come about. Rumours abounded and there was even the suggestion that Williams was not dead, but had absconded with the money.

After his death, an attempt had been made to keep the post of actuary within the Williams family. His grandson was already the clerk at Cardiff and a nephew was in charge of the branch at Aberdare. This did not meet with general approval however, and Mr H J Davies of Bristol was appointed. Mr Williams' grandson, J Ferrier Williams, was re-appointed as clerk.

Then, having heard a rumour from someone connected with the Williams family that he would not last more than three months in his new job, Mr Davies challenged his clerk as to whether everything was in order. The latter, presumably fearing discovery went to one of the bank trustees and confessed that for several years the bank had been defrauded by his grandfather, and that he was aware of how the fraud was committed.

At a hastily convened trustees meeting on 23rd April, the clerk demonstrated how his grandfather had kept two sets of books, had created fictitious accounts, and transacted business outside normal trading hours. In all 18 fraudulent ledgers were found hidden in the attic. Ferrier Williams had known about his grandfather's embezzlement for five years but never had the heart to expose him.

Following further consultation, a decision was made to close the bank. Solicitors were appointed to represent the trustees and managers, accountants appointed to determine the extent of the losses, and a deputation sent to London to discuss the situation with the banking authorities.

Losses were at first thought to exceed £37,000, but after subsequent examination of the books and the sale of the bank premises to Cardiff Council (it was already earmarked for demolition as part of the plan to clear the area next to the castle walls), the deficit was reduced to £29,650.

In all 4,082 individual investors were caught up in the failure, together with 9 Penny Banks, 113 charitable institutions, and 204 Friendly Societies. One of the biggest depositors was St John's church with more than £1,000 invested. It took eight years for the final dividend to be paid, with each account holder receiving at least 17s (85p) in the pound of their original investment.

However, this is more than a story of one dishonest accountant, or the losses sustained by the investors. Within hours of the bank's failure, questions were being raised as to the role of the trustees and managers in the affair, and the extent to which they could be held responsible.

The trustees and managers were drawn from gentlemen of good standing from Cardiff and South Wales whose names would attest to the soundness of the bank. The impressive list was headed by the 3rd Marquess of Bute, as president, and included the Bishops of Llandaff and Bangor, the vicar of St Johns, John Stuart Corbett and numerous aldermen and councillors.

Many of the trustees and managers held their position in name only and had not been involved with the day-to-day running of the banks affairs for many years. For example, Rev W David had become a manager in 1869 but had taken no part in the management for over 20 years, and Mr Corbett, a trustee since 1873, "never took any part worth noticing in the affairs of the bank".

Investigations following the failure revealed that those trustees and managers that did take a day-to-day interest in the running of the bank did so without exercising adequate control. They followed the lax practices that had developed over the years, and trusted the actuary implicitly, countersigning transactions he had conducted without question.

There were obvious calls for the trustees and managers to make up the shortfall. Some of them soon offered to make a contribution, but others declined claiming relative poverty or denying liability.

A test case was eventually brought in 1890 against one of the managers, Peter Davies, who was shown to have countersigned many irregular transactions. Although found liable, a compromise was reached whereby a voluntary payment of £1,000 would release him from any further claims. This served as a benchmark and template for settlement by other trustees and managers, but agreeing who should pay what, if anything, was a messy and often bitter process that went on for several years.

Memorial to James Emerson Williams

Paul Jones

The Marquess of Bute was not a trustee or manager though. He held the position of President, a post he had held since 1848 when he was just six months old, effectively inheriting it from his father. He had attended one meeting when he was 21 and signed the minutes, but was generally ignorant of the company's affairs. Yet his name was on the bank's letterhead, giving added reassurance to potential investors that their money was in safe hands.

Naturally, the liquidators wanted the Marquess to make up the shortfall, but despite his willingness to make a contribution towards the losses along with the trustees a decision was made to bring the case to court. The case was heard in February 1892 before Mr Justice Stirling who ruled in his favour, largely on the grounds that he was entitled to rely on the other trustees and managers to have carried out their own responsibilities and there was no extra duty on him to ensure this.

Not withstanding the judgment, the Marquess of Bute made a sizable contribution to the compensation fund – more than any of the other trustees, and ensured that none of the Friendly Societies that had lost money were out of pocket.

In the summer of 1893, the remaining trustees who had held out against making any contribution reached a compromise and in June 1894, the final dividend was paid to investors.

The failure of the Cardiff Savings Bank was not just of local interest, but made headlines throughout the country. Questions were asked in parliament. It was also a seminal moment in the development of the British banking industry, in so far that it was recognised that the issues raised by the bank's failure needed to be addressed.

Until the Cardiff bank's failure, these "trustee" banks were largely self-administering with little external scrutiny. Yet within a year, the Trustee Savings Bank Association had been created with an aim to protect the interests of depositors, and to increase co-operation between the many savings banks. This association went from strength to strength, culminating in the amalgamation of individual institutions into the TSB in 1976.

This was followed in 1891 by the Savings Bank Act, which tightened up considerably the responsibilities and duties of trustees and directors, and established a regime of inspection.

Even today, there are echoes of the Cardiff Savings Bank failure and in particular the court case against the Marquess of Bute. It is often quoted as an example of UK company case law concerning the duty of care owed by members of a board. In addition, some of the recent problems in the banking industry have highlighted similar issues – the behaviour of individuals in authority and (the lack of) adequate oversight. The case is as relevant today as it was then.

James Emerson Williams lies in a grave in section L of Cathays Cemetery, surrounded in nearby graves by the trustees who had to account for his actions, and the depositors who lost money.

John Farnhill

Simplified Family Tree of Archibald Hood

The Hood family story is told in Chapter 6

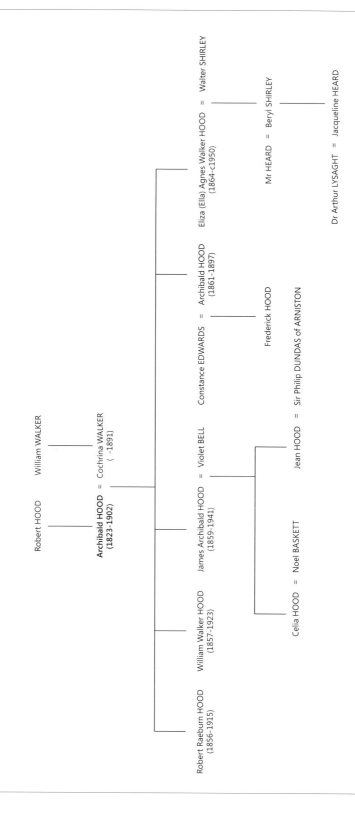

Simplified Cory Family Tree - The Bideford Family

The Cory family story is told in Chapter 10

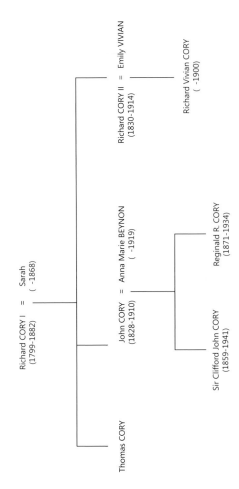

Richard CORY I = Sarah
(1799-1882)   (-1868)

Thomas CORY

John CORY = Anna Marie BEYNON
(1828-1910)   (-1919)

Sir Clifford John CORY
(1859-1941)

Reginald R. CORY
(1871-1934)

Richard CORY II = Emily VIVIAN
(1830-1914)

Richard Vivian CORY
(-1900)

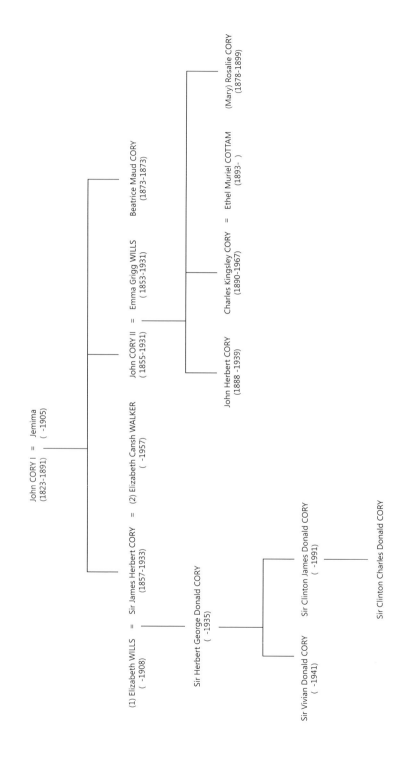

Simplified Cory Family Tree - The Padstow Family

The Cory family story is told in Chapter 10

Index

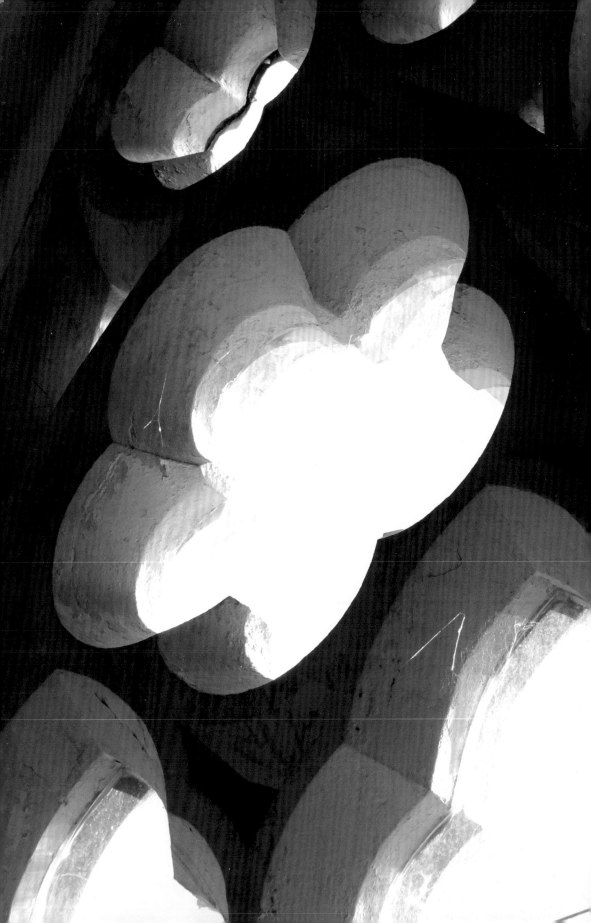